HOW TO RAISE
EMOTIONALLY
HEALTHY CHILDREN

HOW TO RAISE
EMOTIONALLY
HEALTHY CHILDREN

Meeting the Five Critical Needs
of Children . . . And Parents Too!

GERALD NEWMARK, Ph.D.

NMI Publishers
Tarzana, California

NOTE

In this book, we avoid the awkward locutions he/she, him/her. We generally use the more traditional male pronouns which present less stylistic difficulty. The reader should understand that *she* could be substituted for *he* in most instances when it is used in this text to refer to a non-gender noun such as *child*. The same is true of *he* substituting for *she* whenever the latter is used in the same context.

COPYRIGHT © 1999, NMI PUBLISHERS

Eighth Printing

Published by
NMI Publishers
18653 Ventura Boulevard, Suite 547
Tarzana, CA 91356
818-708-1244
nmipub@earthlink.net

Cover Design: Steve Gussman
Cover Photo: Alex Jauregui
Book Design: Tina Hill

Library of Congress Catalog Number: 95-070472

ISBN: 0-932767-07-9

Printed in the United States of America

To my wonderful wife,
Deborah,
who wakes up smiling,
goes to sleep smiling, and
fills my life with
pride and joy.

Contents

ACKNOWLEDGMENTS   ix

FOREWORD   xi

INTRODUCTION   1
(Challenges of Parenting: Pleasures, Paradoxes, Pitfalls)

1. THE FIVE CRITICAL NEEDS OF CHILDREN   9
(Parenting As Though Children *Really* Matter)

2. FAMILY SITUATIONS   39
(A Closer Look at Behavior That Helps and
Behavior That Hurts)

3. RECOLLECTIONS FROM CHILDHOOD   63
(Memories Have Impact)

4. BECOMING A PROFESSIONAL AT PARENTING   73
(Childrearing Is Too Important to Leave to Chance)

**5. OVERCOMING OBSTACLES AND
TAKING CONTROL**   99
(Maintaining Focus and a Balanced Lifestyle)

6. IMPLICATIONS FOR FAMILIES AND SCHOOLS   111
(Creating and Extending a Sense of Community)

7. GUIDE TO PARENT RESOURCES   125
(Tools for Life-Long Learning)

APPENDICES

Appendix A: Family Activities List   135

Appendix B: Daily Journal Form   140

Appendix C: Family Feedback Summary   141

Appendix D: Parent Self-Care Survey   142

Appendix E: Parent Self-Care Evaluation   143

Appendix F: Family Activities Survey   144

Appendix G: Family Activities Evaluation   145

Appendix H: Children's Well-Being Survey   146

Appendix I: Role of Secondary Education in a
Democratic and Changing Society   147

INDEX OF CHAPTER CONTENTS   155

ABOUT THE AUTHOR   163

Acknowledgments

*M*any people contributed to this project at various stages. First and foremost, I extend my sincere gratitude to the children, parents and teachers of three elementary schools in the Los Angeles Unified School District—Pacoima Elementary, Wilshire Crest, and Dublin Ave. schools—all participants in the Tutorial Community Project where the idea for this book first originated. They taught me a great deal about parent-child and teacher-child relations.

I am much indebted to a number of people who read and critiqued one or more drafts. Their comments, suggestions, and anecdotes led to improvements in subsequent drafts. These individuals were: Jan Amsterdam, Kaela Austin, Kathy Cohen, Bill Crawford, Terry David, Denis Girard, Shirley Kessler, Trisha King, Dr. Fred Penrose, Richard Satzman, Dr. Harry Silberman, Gail Zeserman.

Some individuals provided ongoing advice, ideas and encouragement throughout all phases of the project. Their contributions significantly improved the final product and were personally and professionally gratifying to me. They were: Mary Ellen Cassman, Steve Gussman, Dr. Richard Helfant, Dr. Ralph Melaragno, Dan Stein. Numerous and lengthy conversations with Patricia Sun on parenting were inspirational and invaluable.

Thanks to Stan Corwin, my agent, for his advice and belief in the book. The careful editing of Aviva Layton added much to the clarity and conciseness of the book. Thanks also to Frieda Greene and Cynthia Citron for their careful proofreading. Kathy Arft's help in gathering information, checking on details, and typing the final drafts was much appreciated. Special thanks to Steve Gussman for the cover design and as always for his emphasis on getting it right. Many thanks to Tina Hill for her book design and computer typesetting—also for her patience and positive attitude in dealing with last minute changes.

I am very grateful to Dr. Alex Kapelowitz for his book critique and personal counsel during periods of stress. My gratitude also to Dr. Giovanni Aponte and the Meadowbrook staff for their ongoing support and dedication. And to Norman Horowitz, thanks for your friendship, advice, and provocative ideas. My love to Annie Zeserman for who she is and for bringing Deborah into this world. And thanks to my boyhood friends from P.S. 96, P.S. 89, and Columbus High in the Bronx who gave me a sense of community during a childhood that was frequently "trying" but also exhilirating.

To my older, better-looking, richer, smarter and occasionally wiser brother, Irv, thanks for the years of conversation about parenting, where we could identify aspects of our behavior that did not always enhance the emotional health of our children. Also, thanks for your constant love and support which have always been important to me.

To my mother and father, Esther and Joe, my eternal thanks for leaving me with such positive feelings about the importance of family.

To my son, David, my heartfelt gratitude for teaching me important lessons about patience, perseverance, understanding, courage and love in a way that no one else could.

Foreword

With the multitude of books on parenting and child-rearing already at hand, it is both surprising and refreshing to welcome a new one marked by a straightforward and intelligible approach that is as relevant for adults as for the children it addresses. Dr. Newmark challenges the time-honored, emotion-driven, "seat-of-the-pants" approach to parenting, and suggests instead that parents use an intentional, systematized strategy that recognizes and responds to five critical needs of kids. These emotional needs—to feel respected, to feel important, to feel accepted, to feel included, and to feel secure—are neither obscure nor hard to understand. Their importance is obvious. They clearly contribute to self-esteem and self-worth. Yet, as the author abundantly shows, parents' emotional or erratic responses often deny these needs, leaving an accumulating residue of anxiety, self-doubt and uncertainty in the mind of the child.

What is more, these needs are just as important to adults. Unfortunately, in our interactions with each other, they are too often ignored to the detriment of our personal relationships and our own mental health. Can we possibly learn better from our children? It is fitting that Dr. Newmark repeatedly suggests that our children have something to teach us if we will but watch and listen. They frequently have ideas we fail to see as relevant or useful, and express truths that escape us.

This is a book that parents—especially new parents—should have by their bedside. It is a book that child agency personnel and professional caregivers should read and recommend to their clients and patients. Its simple message is one that youth workers should incorporate in their work and that teachers should apply in their classroom. I think parents (and other adults) who successfully practice meeting these critical needs in their children will certainly raise emotionally healthier kids, and as a secondary benefit, hardly less important, significantly improve their own mental health.

Roy W. Menninger, M.D.
Chairman of Trustees,
Menninger Foundation

Introduction

(Challenges of Parenting: Pleasures, Paradoxes, Pitfalls)

As a parent, what a joy it was to wake up in the morning feeling confident that all interactions with my child would be positive and rewarding; that I knew what was needed to develop an emotionally healthy child and how to provide it; that no matter what came up during the day, my behavior would be consistent and positive and that I would rarely feel overwhelmed, frustrated, out-of-control, or at a loss to know what to do.

Further, what a pleasure it was to go to sleep knowing that most of the time I had done the right things that day, and had little or no anxiety or guilt about anything. It was also reassuring to know that if my behavior was "off," I'd be able to recognize it quickly and take corrective action.

How fortunate, too, that my wife and I were in agreement about parenting philosophy and practices and that we would discuss how we were doing on a regular basis, not just when some problem arose. We felt good not to be passive parents, waiting to react to things that went wrong or to problem situations, but rather to be proactively creating a cohesive, happy, dynamic family life. We also realized how wonderful

1

it was for our child to have parents who were relaxed and confident, and who appeared to know what they were doing.

If the above sounds to you like a dream, you are right. That's not the way it was for us, nor is it like that for most parents. For most of us, along with the joy and excitement of parenting, there is much anxiety, insecurity, and inconsistency. Like so many others, our approach to parenting was random, unfocused, and crisis-oriented. Any idea of what parenting could be like at its best or of a thoughtful, systematic approach was unfamiliar to us. As my knowledge, experience and expertise in parent-child relations grew, so did the idea for this book—the notion being to prepare a blueprint that would help parents make the dream described above become a reality. The following thoughts are presented as an introduction to the themes of this book.

Being a parent is one of the greatest joys that one experiences in life, but also one of the most difficult and anxiety-provoking responsibilities any of us will ever have. It is among the most important, challenging and complex tasks a human being has in a lifetime, yet we come to it almost totally unprepared, with little or no training. It is also apparent that once one is a parent, one is a parent forever, and frequently it doesn't get easier over time. I remember my mother saying, "When the kids were little, we had little problems. When they were big, we had big problems."

Parents never stop worrying about their children, no matter how old they are and rarely stop treating them as children, even after they become adults. One of my favorite stories is about arriving at a hotel in Denver and receiving a call from my mother. She called to admonish me to go to bed early because I had a cold when I left Los Angeles. My brother, who was with me on a lecture tour, and who had picked up the phone, responded, "Mom, the kid is 54 years old; he can decide when to go to bed."

There are several things most parents have in common. Clearly, one is that we have all survived childhood—to a greater or lesser extent. Another is that we want our children to survive childhood and prosper as well or better than we have. Third, our intention is to be excellent parents—to do the very best for our children. But usually we underestimate the difficulty of the task. Early on we learn that good intentions and common sense are not enough.

Today, our children are growing up in an age of anxiety, change, and uncertainty—one which is probably more difficult for children than any previous time in history. As an example of this uncertainty, it is said that a current high school senior can expect to change careers—not just jobs, but entire careers—at least 4 times within his lifetime and that 75 percent of these careers do not now exist. We are frightened by the number and seriousness of teenage problems such as suicides and attempted suicides, alcohol and drug abuse, cigarette smoking, sexual promiscuity, school dropouts, crime and violence. And many of these problems now occur during pre-teen years.

Our fears and worries often interfere with giving children what they need. Frequently, we try too hard to protect them and to mold them. We talk, we preach, we scold, we punish, we lecture, we give advice. One minute we threaten them, and the next we shower them with love.

Too often, parents are reactive rather than proactive, correcting something the child has done, rather than consciously striving to create a positive environment that requires less correction. We lack a vision of what parenting could be like at its best and a strategy for achieving it.

The context in which all this takes place is not one where there is a dearth of information on parenting. On the contrary there is a wealth of information—perhaps even an over-abundance—and often contradictory. At times, parents are overwhelmed with too much to assimilate and no overall philosophy or tools to help translate concepts into everyday actions beneficial to children.

Being a parent is not something that you learn once and master for all time. We know that being a parent of a one-year-old is far different from being the parent of a three, five, or ten-year-old, and that being a parent of a teenager is like nothing else. We are not naturally skilled or emotionally prepared for parenting, nor do we automatically get better with experience. When we add to this the constant changes occurring in society, it becomes clear that parents are faced with the challenge of being active lifelong learners.

My basic thesis is that all children have five critical needs that are essential to their emotional health. These are the need to feel respected, important, accepted, included, and secure. When parents understand these basic needs, recognize their importance, and treat childrearing as a professional responsibility, they can develop an overall strategy and a consistent approach to parenting. In so doing, there is an increased likelihood of our becoming the parents we want to be: proactive rather than reactive, appropriately protective rather than overly controlling or permissive, affirming rather than naysaying, consistent rather than haphazard, relaxed rather than tense.

Within this framework, parents will start to master the art of giving children enough freedom so they can grow in their ability to make decisions and become self-reliant, self-confident, independent, thinking people. At the same time, they will be able to provide sufficient structure, guidance, and discipline so children don't harm themselves or grow into self-indulgent, inconsiderate, non-civic-minded individuals.

This book presents a philosophy of parenting and an action-oriented strategy, based on the five critical needs of children, that is designed to achieve emotionally healthy children, parents, and families. This is accomplished by:

- Presenting a vision of what parenting can be at its best: purposeful, systematic, proactive, consistent, self-correcting, inclusive, respectful, positive, loving.

- Providing a philosophy of parenting, a set of core values, that enables parents to interact with children from a sense of conviction and strength.

- Focusing on the five critical needs of children that contribute significantly to their emotional health, and specifying the methods by which parents can satisfy these needs.

- Explaining why common sense and love are necessary and important *but not sufficient,* and defining love in a way that makes it a more meaningful force in parenting.

- Spelling out a strategy that empowers parents to act confidently and consistently in ways that are less stressful and more rewarding to parents and children.

- Providing specific action plans that help even the busiest parents engage in growth experiences with their children and create balanced lifestyles for themselves.

- Giving parents simple, but powerful, tools to measure their effectiveness and make constructive and timely changes.

Children who grow up with this kind of parenting are more likely to:

- Have self-respect and interact with parents and others respectfully.

- Feel important and be able to relate to people and situations with confidence.

- Accept themselves and others and have a positive outlook on life.

- Accept responsibility and take pleasure at being included in, and contributing to, activities and tasks that enhance family life.

- Become self-reliant and able to resist negative influences from peers and society.

- Acquire self-discipline and avoid impulsive, self-destructive actions.

- Openly share joys, anxieties, and problems with parents and be willing to seek information and advice from them.

- Be secure enough to listen to criticism, admit faults and make changes.

- Take advantage of family activities to improve knowledge and skills.

- Build positive relations with siblings and peers.

To write this book, I have relied on several sources. Initial concepts came from my personal experience, analyzing relations and interactions as a child with my own parents and as a parent with my own child, and as a teacher with my students and their parents. From these initial reflections I began to formulate some general ideas, and many questions, about the needs of children and behavior of parents which thwarted or satisfied these needs.

These ideas started to coalesce during the seven years I was co-director of a Ford Foundation-supported project to create a model elementary school in the Los Angeles City Schools. In working closely with teachers, parents and children, it became apparent that some adults were more effective with children than others. Seeking to find out what accounted for these differences, I started to observe parent-child interactions more closely, followed by extended conversations with parents, teachers, and children. At this stage, my concept of the five critical needs of children began to crystallize.

Out of this, I developed a series of lectures and seminars on parent-child relations which were sponsored by school, religious, and civic groups. Confirmation of the concept of the five critical needs of children emerged from interviews with, and questionnaires completed by, several hundred young people and parents attending these sessions. The material and conclusions presented here represent a synthesis of these experiences and a lifetime of observation and study.

This book was written for parents of children of all ages, infants through teen years, and expectant parents too. It also has special significance for teachers and schools, and for all others involved in the education and care of children. At its core, it is about enhancing the emotional health of children, parents, and families; about moving rapidly and thoughtfully from concepts to action and about positive, pleasurable, parenting. It's about parenting as though children *really* matter! And parents too!

The Five Critical Needs of Children

(Parenting as Though Children Really Matter)

*A*s previously stated, parenting is not something you learn once and master for all time; children at different ages have different needs, and parents must learn to adjust their approach accordingly. To be a good parent, one must be a good learner and our children are frequently our best teachers, if we take the time to listen and learn from them. Although different ages and different personalities require different understandings, I believe there are five critical needs that all children, at all ages, have in common—the need to feel respected, important, accepted, included, and secure. I call these needs "critical" because when satisfied they are the key to developing an emotionally healthy child. They serve parents as a road map to guide their actions, assess progress, build on strengths and overcome shortcomings. These guidelines, and the action plans which accompany them, increase the probability of parents becoming better at parenting each successive year.

Need to Feel Respected

Children need to feel respected. For that to happen, they need to be treated in a courteous, thoughtful, attentive, and civil manner—as individuals, deserving of the same courtesy and considerateness as others. When I was growing up, I heard over and over again, "Treat your parents with respect, and your teachers and older people, too." And that's fine; we need to say these things, but one of the best ways for children to learn about respect is to feel what it's like to be treated respectfully and to observe their parents and other adults treating each other the same way.

It is curious how many parents treat their children in ways that they objected to when they were children. In spite of parents knowing better, conditioning is frequently hard to overcome. Children need to be treated with the respect that we ourselves would welcome. For example, it is just as easy and takes the same amount of time to say, "I'm sorry honey. I don't have time right now," rather than to say, "Can't you see I'm busy? Stop bothering me!" The impact on the child of each statement is significantly different—with children a simple act of courtesy can go a long way.

Parents' opinions, values, attitudes, and actions matter to children—even to teenagers who sometimes pretend not to care. Discourtesy, rudeness, inconsiderateness on the part of adults is often the result of thoughtlessness. We don't think of children as having the same needs as adults, and we do not realize the effect we have on them by what we say and how we say it.

When children are treated with respect, they will feel good about themselves and will be more likely to act respectfully towards others, including their own children when they become parents.

The following are some areas where there is considerable room for improvement in how we relate to children.

RUDENESS, DISCOURTESY

While visiting a friend who was having a conversation with his eight-year-old son, the telephone rang; although the child was speaking at the moment, the father abruptly got up and without saying a word took the call, engaging the caller in a lengthy conversation. When the child walked over to him and tried to finish what he had been saying, the father frowned and said in a loud voice, "Don't be rude. Can't you see I'm talking?" Now I ask you, who was really rude in this situation?

Upon hearing the phone ring, how would it have been if the father had said to his son, "Excuse me, Bobby. Let me see who that is. I'll be right back." And what if he had said to the caller, "I'm sorry, I'll have to call you back. I'm having a conversation with my son." Not only would that have been respectful, but think how important it might have made the child feel.

One day, while working for a research corporation, my work wasn't going well; discouraged, I left early. When I arrived home and walked into the kitchen, my son was already home from school. He was having corn flakes and milk, and I noticed the refrigerator door had been left open. I started scolding him about how thoughtless he was and how all the food in the refrigerator would spoil and how we couldn't afford that kind of waste. Suddenly David started to cry.

"What are you crying about?" I shouted.

"I didn't do it on purpose; you act like I'm some sort of criminal," he replied.

"Oh, you big baby," I exclaimed, and left the house.

I took a short walk to calm down, and realized that my reaction was out of proportion to what had happened and that it really had nothing to do with either my son or the refrigerator. It had to do with the way I was feeling about myself and how my work was going. I was acting as though the last thing this kid did, every night before he went to sleep, was to make a list—"How Many Ways Can I Make My Father Miserable Tomorrow." Of course that was not the case, but my tone of voice and entire manner did imply that he had committed a serious offense. At the very least, I was certainly not treating him with respect. Realizing this, I went back into the house and apologized.

Another day while I was observing activities at a school during yard recess, I noticed a teacher shouting at a child who was walking along bouncing a ball. The teacher said, "Where are you going with that ball? The ball should be put away; recess is over. Come over here right now." The child turned her back and walked away from the teacher without answering. The teacher ran over to the child, grabbed her by the shoulder and said, "Don't you dare turn your back on me!" and took her to the principal's office. The principal scolded the child for being disobedient and then asked, "Why did you act that way? Why didn't you do what the teacher said?" To which the child responded simply, "I didn't like the way she talked to me." Yes, children have feelings too.

LYING

Another way in which we don't treat children with respect is by lying to them. When we lie to children, we lose credibility. We give them the impression that lying is OK, that maybe adults do not feel they have to be truthful with children.

It starts with little things, like saying to a child, "This is for your own good" when we know well that it's really for our own convenience, or when we make a promise and don't keep it or try to lie our way out of it. By so doing, we lose the opportunity to help children gain insights into lying. And later, when we punish them for lying, we compound the problem.

Once when visiting a private school, I remember seeing a child wearing a sign, "I am a liar." I stopped him and asked why he was wearing the sign.

He answered, "I'm being punished for lying."

Playing devil's advocate, I asked, "What's wrong with lying?"

"When you lie, you usually get caught and get punished."

"Well, suppose you didn't get caught, would it be all right to lie?"

"I guess so," was his response.

One newspaper described the extent of the problem by stating that lying had become so prevalent in American society that most people don't know when they are lying or telling the truth anymore.

At an unconscious level—at least—the inner tension must be great for children who want to believe their parents are paragons of virtue, and yet see through some of their lies. It is frequently startling and sometimes disturbing when, as we get older, we realize that our parents are fallible human beings with numerous shortcomings. With children especially, honesty is still the best policy!

DEMEANING BEHAVIOR

If, when children make mistakes or don't do what we want them to do, we call them names (dumb, stupid, lazy, greedy, selfish) or otherwise belittle them by word, tone, or action, we are acting disrespectfully. The parents' goal should be to try to understand why the child is acting inappropriately and

seek effective ways to help the child behave in more constructive ways. Inappropriate or exaggerated anger, impatience, or
sarcasm creates defensiveness or retaliatory behavior by the
child. In this situation, little learning takes place either in the
parent or child. For example, to say sarcastically to an 11th
grader who is not showing enough interest in school that
he should look for an after-school job washing dishes "because that's all you'll be good for if you don't go to college"
is both counterproductive and disrespectful. To tell a teenager that her lipstick and dress make her look like a tramp
will not encourage her to use you as a consultant on personal
grooming.

INTERRUPTING/IGNORING/HALF-LISTENING

We treat children with disrespect when we don't listen to
them, when we are easily distracted, when we don't give them
our attention, when we ignore them. This occurs when a child
says something and we don't respond, or we change the
subject without alluding to the child's remark; frequently, we
interrupt to tell her to do something. Sometimes a friend or
relative will ask a child, "How are you doing in school,
Annie?" and before she can respond, we jump in and answer
for her. In each case, we are acting disrespectfully.

SUMMING UP

If we want children to grow up with self-respect and to be
respectful of others, we need to be courteous, considerate and
respectful of them. We need to avoid sarcasm, belittling,
yelling; we need to keep anger and impatience to a minimum;
we need to stop lying to them; we need to listen more and
talk less; we need to treat them not as things to be controlled
and manipulated but rather as people to relate to. We need
to command less and suggest more. We need to learn how to

say "please," "thank you," and "excuse me"—yes, even to children. We need to remember that children have feelings too, and that how we say something is as important as what we say. This does not mean that as parents we must be saints, or that we don't make demands on children. As long as we understand the need for children to be treated with respect and have a vision of what a respectful relationship looks like, we shall continue to make progress, and both child and parent will benefit.

Need to Feel Important

Feeling important includes a child's need to have a sense of value, power, control, usefulness; to feel that "I am somebody." This need is evident at a very early age. I recall observing a small child in an elevator, whose mother was about to press the floor button. The child shouted, "No, no, me, me!" and struggled on her tiptoes to press the button. On another occasion, when I tried to help a child adjust his seat belt, he responded indignantly, "I'll do it myself."

If children do not feel important and useful (and this is a major problem for our young people today), if they don't develop a sense of importance in constructive ways, they may seek negative ways to get attention. They may become rebellious, outrageous, antagonistic; they may engage in constant testing and struggling for power; they may join cliques or gangs, and they may turn to drugs, sex, crime, or violence. At the other extreme, they may become apathetic or withdrawn; they may lack initiative and ambition or they may become overly dependent on others.

One of the greatest challenges for parents, families and communities is to find ways to help children develop this sense of importance, self-worth, usefulness and identity.

OVERPROTECTIVENESS

Parents diminish a child's sense of power by limiting them too much. I, for one, was overprotective as a parent to an exaggerated degree. As a child growing up in New York City with both parents working, I had a lot of freedom. I ran the streets, and many times felt lonely and frightened; because of that, many years later, I decided unconsciously that my son was never going to feel that way. Guided by my fears, I went to the other extreme and became overprotective. I wanted to know what he was doing, where he went, and who he was with every minute of the day. It was not in my son's best interest and certainly not in mine. His mother also parented out of excess fear. It created considerable rebellion in our household.

Children need to experiment; they need to try things. That's the way they learn and grow; that's the way their sense of power grows. We need to encourage rather than inhibit their curiosity, their interest in experimentation, their desire for adventure. We say "no" to children too often. Children need many more "yes's" than "no's." Certainly, we need to take measures to protect our children from realistic danger, but also must determine if we have imagined or exaggerated potential danger and gone too far in being protective.

EXCESSIVE PERMISSIVENESS

The other side of being overly protective is being too permissive. Yes, kids need more "yes's" than "no's" when they are growing up, but if you never or rarely say "no," children could be in trouble. They may have unrealistic expectations and believe that anything is permissible. Their immaturity may cause them to take inappropriate or unsafe risks.

Children should participate in establishing limits and be listened to with an open mind. If parents realize that the risks have been exaggerated, they should be willing to back off. On the other hand, some things may not be negotiable, such as smoking, using drugs, drinking. Even then, when children are part of the decision process and their opinions are heard, it will contribute to their sense of importance. When left to do whatever they want, children often feel abandoned.

TALKING TOO MUCH/NOT LISTENING

Parents often contribute to a child's sense of powerlessness by talking too much and not listening enough. We talk; we lecture; we give advice; we tell them how to feel and what to think; we overpower them with words when we should be listening more to what they are thinking and feeling. Not listening says to the child, "I am not interested in what you have to say, you are not important enough for me to listen to." Listening says, "I care about what you have to say. You are important to me."

One of the most valuable assets in interpersonal relations—which too few people possess—is the ability to give someone you are with your undivided attention, the feeling of being the most important person in the world at that moment. It is especially important with children to listen actively and to be fully present. This does not necessarily require an inordinate amount of time. Even if you have only two or three minutes to spend with a child, you can put other things aside and give the child your total attention—acting as though for those few minutes there is no one in the world more important.

When we listen to children, we not only give them a sense of importance, but they will want to listen more to us. And, the more we listen, the more we learn about them so that we can interact in positive, constructive ways.

DECISION MAKING/PROBLEM SOLVING

When parents are all knowing, all powerful—making all decisions and solving all problems—children do not grow in self-esteem and self-confidence. Involving children in decision-making and problem solving, asking their opinions and listening to their answers, contributes to their sense of "I am somebody."

People do not suddenly, at a certain age magically develop good judgment and become good decision makers. They become good at making bigger and better decisions by having experience at making smaller decisions along the way.

There are innumerable opportunities to involve children in decision-making at every age level. Whether it is about solving a family problem, preparing a menu for a family meal, planning a family activity, deciding what clothes to wear for different occasions, or caring for a pet, children can be involved.

In addition to helping children feel important, you will be pleasantly surprised at what comes out of their mouths. One father, when discussing over dinner his desire to change jobs because he was unhappy with his present position, asked his teenage children what they thought. His daughter inquired why he was unhappy and after he mentioned the reasons, she responded, "How do you know it will be any different somewhere else?" The ensuing discussion caused him to stop and think; he had not really taken his best shot at changing conditions where he was, or at looking at his own weaknesses which contributed to his present unhappiness. His daughter's question made him realize that his problems could very well follow him to the next place.

RESPONSIBILITY/AUTHORITY

Don't do everything for your children. Share tasks, household chores, responsibilities, authority. From the earliest age, gradually provide them with more and more complex tasks to perform both for themselves and for the family. And, along with responsibilities, give them appropriate status (e.g., authority and titles). For example, in one family where a child had the responsibility to care for the family dog, the child had the title of Director of Animal Husbandry. She was also asked to prepare and administer an expense budget for the animal. Once the budget was approved by the parents, the daughter was given full control.

Another family appointed one of their children as Safety Director. Under the latter's direction, a safety checklist was prepared along with a rotating inspection schedule shared by all family members. An older child asked to read nightly to a younger sibling was called "Tutor." As an "Assistant Chef" a child could learn lifelong skills while being a big help to parents in the kitchen. Every child in the family could end up having a major responsibility and a title to go with it, and these can be rotated from time to time.

Many areas of family life afford opportunities for children to participate and contribute in a meaningful way. These responsibilities not only enhance the child's sense of importance and power, but can also serve as excellent learning tools for developing reading, writing, math, problem solving and research skills.

SUMMING UP

Parents need to avoid being all powerful, solving all family problems, making all decisions, doing all the work, controlling everything that happens. Involve your children—ask their opinions; give them things to do; share decision-making and power; give them status and recognition, and have patience with mistakes when it takes a little longer or is not done as well as you could have done it yourself.

Children need to feel powerful, important, useful. If you give children constructive, meaningful ways to feel important and treat them as though they are, they will not need to "act out" in order to attempt to convince themselves and others that "I am somebody."

Need to Feel Accepted

Children have a need to be accepted as individuals in their own right, with their own uniqueness, and not treated as mere reflections of their parents, as objects to be shaped in the image of what parents believe their ideal child should look like.

This means that children have a right to their own feelings, opinions, desires, and ideas. We need to recognize that feelings are not right or wrong; they just are. Acceptance does not imply liking or agreeing, nor does it have anything to do with accepting or condoning behavior. In fact, confusing feelings and desires with behavior is one of the problems parents have. Accepting a child's feelings is simply recognition that like all individuals, children have feelings too, and that a child's feelings are not to be suppressed or feared but rather to be understood, discussed, and worked with when necessary.

If feelings are trivialized or put down, it could raise self doubts in children or a tendency to close up. If we don't listen to their feelings, they may fester and surface later as inappropriate or destructive behavior. There is also less chance that children will come to us for help with problems.

OVERREACTING/EMOTIONALITY

At a workshop for teenagers, an 18-year-old high school senior related the following interaction with his parents: When asking for permission to join several friends for an overnight sleepout on the Santa Monica beach following their senior prom, his father replied, "What, are you crazy! Don't you know how many muggings there are in Los Angeles?" His mother joined in, "It's out of the question." According to the son, both parents abruptly walked out of the room without waiting for a response.

This emotional reaction on the part of the parents was obviously motivated by fear of their son engaging in what they perceived as a dangerous activity—something that any parent might easily identify with. But they acted as though they were being presented with a *fait accompli,* rather than a request. Their hasty, negative response was insensitive to the son's feelings and to the effect this rejection—both the substance and the form—might have on him. The rhetorical parental response, "What, are you crazy!" implies that there is something wrong with someone who has such a desire.

A parent who accepts the child's right to his desires, and is not overcome by fear and emotion, responds differently. For example, "Yes, I guess it would be exciting, but I have some reservations; with the kind of crimes that are occurring these days, it would make me very nervous. Let's think about it, and we'll discuss it some more." By accepting the child's desire, we can prevent bad feelings from developing. Since we are considerate of the child's feelings, we can discuss the situation with a greater probability of finding an amicable solution—either by easing the parents' fears or having the child accept an alternative suggestion.

Fear often causes parents to confuse possibility with probability. Because something is possible, we frequently act as though it is probable—that it will happen. This is an important distinction for parents to keep in mind. By realizing that many things we fear are highly improbable, we may be inclined to say "yes" more often and worry less.

In a workshop for parents, a mother related the following story:

Her child had received a bicycle for Christmas; a month later they were shopping at a mall when the child, noticing a better quality bike in a store window exclaimed, "Gee, would I like to have that one!" The mother retorted, "You ungrateful child! You just got a new bicycle for Christmas; how can you be so greedy." She went on and on, yet the child was only expressing a desire. Another parent related that in a similar situation with another gift, she had simply said, "Yes, I guess it would be nice to have the latest model. Do you know why you can't have it?" The child replied, "Sure, because I just got one." Very often we overreact without thinking, and hold children to a higher standard than we ourselves can meet. Haven't we, as adults, sometimes regretted a purchase after seeing something more desirable a few weeks later?

When parent behavior is governed by fear, emotionality or irrationality, an opportunity is lost for a positive, constructive parent-child interaction.

SUPPRESSING FEELINGS

We often do children a disservice by attempting to talk them out of their feelings. The child is upset because a friend is mad at him and the parent says, "Don't be stupid; he's not worth thinking about. Anyway, you have plenty of other friends." Now the child feels twice as bad—first because the friend is still mad at him and then because the parent suggests he may be stupid for feeling bad. The parent may be well-intentioned, not wanting the child to be unhappy; sometimes the parent is frustrated, feeling that the child is too sensitive to what other kids think. The parent wants to fix things, make everything okay, make nice, protect the child from feeling hurt—that's a parent's job, isn't it?

But the parent's statement misses the mark. The message conveyed is not comforting or enlightening. It may convey the idea that being upset when something negative happens is bad. In addition to causing discomfort for the child, it is a conversation stopper, and denies the child an opportunity to explore his feelings and perhaps learn how to handle them in a constructive way.

A parent who understands that feelings aren't right or wrong, and that the child has a right to his own feelings, won't try to talk him out of them. Acting in this light, a parent may respond by saying: "I guess it hurts when a good friend is mad at you." The parent might also identify with the child, recalling similar feelings when the parent was a child. Here the message is that it's perfectly okay to have these feelings. The child's distress may be of very short duration in any case, and might have disappeared quickly, even had the parent said nothing.

Parents don't always have to do something about a child's hurt feelings. Just being there may be enough to comfort the child. When a child's bad feelings persist and are affecting the child's life negatively, the parent can help the child explore those feelings and consider different ways of handling them. How much better than having a child be ashamed of feelings, bury them, and have them come out in negative ways.

BEING OVERLY CRITICAL

Another barrier to satisfying the need to be accepted is when parents criticize their children excessively, constantly giving them negative feedback. When this happens, children may develop a low opinion of themselves, tune out the criticism, or feel defeated. "What's the use, I'll never satisfy them," may become the child's attitude. An elementary school child once alluded to this negative emphasis when responding to a question about discipline in her school: "If you're acting okay, the teacher never notices you, but if you're misbehaving she'll spend hours with you."

We need to overlook many things. There is a saying in business that applies to parenting as well, "Don't sweat the small stuff." We don't have to react to everything.

POSITIVE REINFORCEMENT

We should be emphasizing the positive—praising the child, looking for things to acknowledge. In a best-selling, management book, *The One Minute Manager,* by Kenneth Blachard and Spencer Johnson, a major point is the need to "catch people doing something right and tell them about it." We are very good at catching people, especially children, doing something wrong, and need to change the emphasis to catching them doing something right. Children especially need more acknowledgments than put downs. If we look for occasions to praise, we will find them. And as we praise more, such occasions will multiply. When having to criticize, focus on the behavior and not the person. Learn how to reject with love and not with anger. For example, "I'm sure it would be exciting to spend the night on the beach with your friends, and I hate to disappoint you by saying no, but it would make me too nervous," rather than "What, are you crazy!"

SUMMING UP

Accepting children means listening, trying to understand them, and accepting their right to their point of view, feelings, desires, opinions, and ideas. If you act in a way that tells them they have no right to feel or think something, you imply there is something wrong with them; you reduce the chance of their listening to you and of your being able to influence their behavior positively. Acceptance is not permissiveness. It's not giving children free license to act in any way they wish. On the contrary, it should reduce inappropriate behavior. Acceptance increases the likelihood of avoiding adversarial relations and power struggles.

Accept your children as people in their own right and act accordingly. Recognize their accomplishments; don't sweat the small stuff; emphasize the positive; when you must say no, do so with love. Don't let exaggerated fears govern the relationship with your children. Remember, just because something might happen does not mean it will.

Need to Feel Included

Children need to be included. They need to be brought in, to be made to feel a part of things. Children often feel left out and unwanted; when this happens they feel as if they are outsiders rather than part of the family. How often do they hear, "Not now, you'll have to wait until you're older." "You're only a child, this is not for you."

People who do things together feel closer to one another. Family activities offer a way of becoming closer and also of having fun, learning, and contributing to others. Identifying strongly with the family unit makes children more resistant to outside negative influences and more open to positive role models within the family.

Obviously, children can't be included in everything, but we need to make a conscious effort to include them in as many ongoing family activities as possible. And, when not included in something they want to be a part of, an explanation by the parent is helpful.

ACTIVITIES

Childhood is a time of curiosity and experimentation. Family activities can be used to have children try new things, broaden their interests, and strengthen their relations with other family members. There are any number of activities in which all family members can participate and enjoy. (See Appendix A, *Family Activities List*—a comprehensive list of over 150 different activities.)

WORKLIFE ACTIVITY

Including children in your worklife has multiple benefits. Describe to them where you work, what you do, with whom you work, and how you feel about your work and your fellow workers. Include anything that will help them better understand that part of your life. If possible, take them to your workplace, introduce them to co-workers, show them your office. Encourage them to ask questions and find out what they think about their visit—what impressed them, what they learned. If you work at home or have your own business, introduce them to clients and co-workers, and possibly have them do some work for you.

Since work is such an important part of your life, your children will feel more connected to you. They will learn about an entirely different aspect of you. And, when you and your spouse discuss something that happened at work, they will probably show more interest and be able to learn from the way you face situations and challenges.

DECISIONS

The family is a community whose well-being is dependent, like that of other groups, on the quality of its decisions, cooperation of its members, sense of belonging, and positive feelings of regard for one another. People learn, grow, and participate best in an environment where they have some control and know that what they say or do counts. This applies to children too. Obviously, in the family community, parents are the leaders. To the extent that children participate in decisions, there will be greater commitment to carry them out and to make them work.

Whenever possible we need to ask our children's opinions, give them choices and explain decisions at a level appropriate to their age and maturity. This is the way children learn and grow in their own decision-making ability and confidence. Opportunities for children to participate in decision-making are endless and present themselves on a daily basis.

DISCUSSIONS

Children are frequently left out of conversations and discussions because the subject matter is for adults only. While this is often true, at times we may be overly exclusive; we need to involve children more in conversations where information and feelings about what's happening in the family are shared. This means shielding them less from family concerns and problems. Too often we underestimate what children can handle.

FAMILY FEEDBACK MEETINGS

It is beginning to be recognized that children need opportunities to discuss their concerns, feelings, problems in an open, supportive climate. This includes the opportunity for children to learn about constructive criticism—not only how to receive the most benefit from it but also how to offer it effectively so others will listen. Their participation in efforts to improve family communication and understanding can yield many benefits.

Some families have started family feedback sessions on a regular basis in which everyone can discuss things that are going on in their lives. In one such session, Sally, a divorced working mother, met with her three children, Pamela 12, Robert 11, and Tony 7. She started the meeting by sharing her guilt feelings at not spending enough time with her kids. Robert responded by agreeing that she was neglecting them, and that she had too many outside activities. Pamela felt that Robert should stop complaining and help his mother more. Tony was quiet. Sally reviewed with them her activities outside the family—her job, church and occasional social activities. Robert reminded her that she had left out an important category. When Sally asked him to be specific, he responded by saying, "Miscellaneous, you are being 'miscellaneoused' to death." Further discussion supported Robert. Sally was constantly being asked to participate on various work, church, political and civic committees and had a hard time saying "no." As a result of this meeting, she reconsidered her priorities and made some changes in her lifestyle.

In one elementary school, where 2nd grade class feedback meetings were held weekly, one teacher asked the children what she had done that week that they liked or didn't like. One of the kids said that he was upset when a girl in his class cried.

"Why were you upset?" the teacher inquired.

"Well, I don't like when people cry—only girls and babies cry, and you should have stopped her."

"Do any of you boys ever feel like crying?" the teacher asked.

"I feel like crying sometimes, when my parents get angry with me," one child replied.

"And do you cry then?" asked the teacher.

"Oh, no," replied the boy, "only girls and babies cry."

At which point, one little boy in the back of the room raised his hand and said, "I think girls cry on the outside and boys cry on the inside." Out of the mouths of babes!

These sessions can create an atmosphere where children are more willing to share their fears, concerns, and questions about growing up, school, health, sex, and other subjects, which children typically might be embarrassed or reticent to discuss with parents, and where parents might also be more willing to share family problems. In this way, these sessions contribute to children feeling included as an integral part of the family, and they also learn to appreciate their parents more realistically as people.

SUMMING UP

Children need to be included, to feel "in" on things. Make a conscious decision to include children in as many decisions, discussions and activities as possible, appropriate to their maturity and the family situation. Don't leave it to chance; make a plan, and involve the children in the planning. Select activities that all family members will find interesting and worthwhile, either as a total group or with two or more participants.

Need to Feel Secure

Security means providing children with a stable, consistent, safe and caring environment, in which they feel protected and loved and where the intentions and behavior of people have their best interests at heart.

The art of childrearing involves maintaining a balance between freedom and control. Children need limits; without limits, they will not feel secure or safe. They will be apprehensive, exposed to danger and not protected from their own impulses and inexperience. However, too many limits, too much rigidity, inconsistent discipline, and excessive punishment leave children confused and rebellious and don't allow for the security of self-discipline.

Above all, children need to be in a positive environment where people get along, care about one another, and consistently express warmth and love in words and actions.

RELATIONSHIP OF PARENTS WITH EACH OTHER

At the end of a seminar for parents in which we had discussed the five critical needs of children, one parent remarked, "Wow, what a revelation—my husband and I have these same needs." The group consensus was that if couples treated each other with these five needs in mind, there would be happier marriages, fewer divorces and more secure, joyful children.

For children, parents are their primary role models. When parents bicker a lot, treat each other disrespectfully and rarely show affection, children experience insecurity and anxiety. As one person said, "I used to see my parents argue and fight. That wouldn't have been so bad, except that I never saw them make up. It was unsettling." Some children have felt that their parent's negativity towards each other reflected how they felt about them, or that they were somehow the cause of their parents not getting along. One of the most significant things a parent can do for a child's sense of security is to act in a way so that the other spouse feels respected, important, accepted, included, and secure.

A CARING, AFFECTIONATE ENVIRONMENT

Among other things, a caring environment is one in which family members show affection towards one another. Seeing affection between parents and receiving affection from them is very important to the child's sense of security.

Beginnings and endings are especially important. How you begin and end the day, week, month and year presents opportunities for regular demonstrations of affection. One parent shared with us how her mother always awakened her in the morning with a hug and a kiss, while another bemoaned the fact that she usually awakened her own children by yelling such admonitions as "Hurry up and get out of bed or you'll be late for school," "If you don't make your bed before coming down to breakfast, you'll get no money for dessert with your lunch." Showing affection—hugs, kisses, smiles, terms of endearment—at the beginning and end of the day and after other intervals of not seeing one another, contributes to a warm, positive family atmosphere, especially when not mixed in with lots of instructions, lectures and nagging. And, of course, spontaneous expressions of affection, whenever the spirit moves you, are always desirable.

TRADITION AND RITUALS

Established traditions and rituals to celebrate events give children a sense of stability and security. In addition to the usual holiday and birthday celebrations, one can involve children in establishing others. For example, one could schedule a weekly or monthly dinner at which family members share something for which they feel particularly thankful. Another example would be a discussion dinner where some special topic is explored: each person brings in a story to share and discuss, e.g., current events, human interest, sports.

DISCIPLINE

Responsibility for Actions

Parents need to discuss with children why certain behaviors are inappropriate or irresponsible, and that such behavior on their part will usually cause unpleasant consequences for them. For example, one parent upon discovering that her son had shop-lifted a toy from a store didn't say too much to the child—simply that "in our family we don't take things from each other without permission, nor do we steal things from others." She then—to the child's considerable chagrin—accompanied the boy to the store to return the toy to the manager and apologize. The manager accepted the apology and explained that if it happened again he would have to call the police.

Excessive Limits

Setting arbitrary, inflexible limits, without a rationale that is understandable to the child or without any discussion or involvement of the child, frequently results in a tug-of-war which makes compliance difficult and leaves both parent and child insecure. The following are examples of rules difficult to maintain with the average 14-year-old child:

- Must be in bed by 9 p.m.

- Can't spend allowance on snacks.

- No watching TV during the week.

- No telephone calls, except on weekends.

Excessive/Inappropriate Punishment

Such punishment is usually difficult to enforce, is frequently viewed by the child as unjust, and consequently provides little learning as the child is preoccupied with the unfairness of the situation. The result may be acting out by the child and a state of tension between parent and child. The examples below often occur when parents are angry:

- Didn't do homework one day—grounded for 2 week-ends.

- Broke telephone curfew rule—can't use telephone for 3 weeks.

- Lost an item of clothing—no TV for 10 days.

Inconsistent Punishment

When we constantly threaten and don't follow through, the child is confused or disbelieving, and we lose credibility. Once at our condominium a guest informed his son that he needed to get out of the swimming pool as they were leaving in 15 minutes. About 15 minutes later the father was shouting, "If you don't get out of the pool by the time I count to ten, we're leaving without you." At the count of ten, the father repeated the count twice more, each time stating this was the child's last chance, and adding another threat.

When one parent is lenient and the other strict, it is confusing for the child. When parents disagree with each other unpleasantly in front of the child, the latter's security is threatened. The child is more secure when parents say what they mean, mean what they say, appear united and seem to know what they are doing.

Physical Punishment

Physical punishment needs to be avoided. It deals with symptoms and often delays or even prevents solutions. The wrong lessons may be learned. When we hit a child, sometimes the lesson might be that it's all right to use force if you are bigger and stronger. Reactions to force are sometimes delayed, but strong. The kid who is paddled by the principal can't do anything immediately, but he might come back on the weekend and vandalize the school. After being spanked by a parent, a child may take it out on a younger sibling or schoolmate.

There is no security if you don't learn from the situation. The medium may confound the message; physical force may distract a child from learning. Ideally, punishment should be established with the child's participation, be appropriate to the situation, administered firmly with love, and provide some insight to the child. It should be thought of in terms of a learning process rather than punishment designed merely to hurt.

Self-Discipline

Self-discipline must be encouraged and developed. This means allowing children to explore and experience the consequences of their actions, so that they learn to anticipate negative consequences and exercise self-control to avoid them. Too much control deprives children of this opportunity.

SUMMING UP

Parents must realize that children need freedom as much as control; to squelch or smother children can result in intimidated, withdrawn children or frustrated, rebellious ones. One of our goals is to protect them so they don't suffer from their inexperience; another is for them to grow into confident, self-reliant, self-directed individuals.

Growing up in a positive, caring environment contributes to a child's sense of security. Seeing parents in a loving, respectful relationship is of utmost importance.

Children also need limits and discipline that are appropriate, reasonable, and consistent. Consequences for exceeding or ignoring limits should be enforceable and not punishing to the parents. Adversarial relations or power struggles leave both parent and child frustrated and insecure. Involve the children when establishing rules and consequences for violations; it increases the likelihood of their working.

When parents interact with each other and their children in ways that satisfy the children's five critical needs, the need for discipline is greatly reduced, and self-discipline is more likely to grow and develop.

What About Love?

You perhaps have asked yourself, "What about love? Why hasn't love been included as one of the five critical needs of children?" It was omitted purposefully, not because it lacks importance—on the contrary, it is extremely important—but rather because the word "love" has become ambiguous, and has lost some of its force and meaning.

In many cases, saying the words "I love you" has become trite, meaningless, or confusing. In an interview with a young woman, she relates the following conversation with her mother from whom she has been estranged for some time: The mother says to the daughter, "You know we love you sweetheart, don't you? Didn't we always tell you we loved you?" To which the daughter replies angrily, "Love, what do you know about love? You told me you loved me, but you never showed me you did."

There are parents who abuse or neglect their children and then say "I love you," thinking it makes up for their behavior. Too often, love is equated with saying "I love you." If saying "I love you" were enough, we might not have such a high divorce rate. Marriages don't break up because a spouse stops saying "I love you." They break up because spouses quit treating each other in a loving way—their behavior is not loving and consequently it becomes harder and harder to believe in the words "I love you."

Most parents love their children—that's a given; however, we cannot assume from this that most parents act in a loving way. One mother recalled being reassured by a prominent childrearing expert that if you loved your child and were authentic and honest, your child would turn out just fine.

Love, honesty, and authenticity are certainly significant concepts, but "all that glitters is not gold." I'm reminded of a father who constantly berated and belittled his son, calling him fat, lazy, stupid and many other things. The son, now an adult, still suffers from the effects of that relationship. Yet, the father loved his son, was honest about his feelings, and was being authentic.

So, my answer to "What about love?" is that loving your child is essential and saying "I love you" is important, but neither is sufficient unless you act in a loving way. That is why I think about love as a verb, and define "acting in a loving way" as relating to children in ways that promote their well-being. Emotional health is acting in a way to ensure that the child feels respected, important, accepted, included, and secure—that's the best way to say "I love you."

Concluding Thoughts

Examples of adults interacting with children in the manner illustrated above have become commonplace. Parents need to become aware of this and have the desire to do something about it, if progress is to be made in meeting children's emotional needs.

Understanding the five critical needs of children provides the basis for parenting that is forward-looking and action-oriented. This approach applies to children of all age groups and segments of society, despite individual differences. It provides parents with a concrete framework to guide their interactions with children, and gives them a practical tool for evaluating how things are going.

Above all, enjoy your children; have fun with them and the experience of parenting. When your behavior is "off" in some way—you lose your cool, you make a mistake, you do something you wish you hadn't—don't be hard on yourself. Don't expect to be perfect. Relax! It's part of being human.

Remember, having happy, relaxed parents is a great gift we can give to our children. Be kind to yourself. Be good to one another. Create time for yourselves so that you feel nourished and in good spirits. Appreciate and enjoy the wonder of this great adventure called parenting.

The concept of the five needs of children makes the parenting task much easier. Children have these five needs throughout their lives. So, although children at different ages and stages of development may act differently, have different problems, and express their personalities in particular ways, these five needs remain constant. This enables parents to apply the principles of the five needs under all circumstances and in all situations. It gives parents continuous practice in relating to children in emotionally healthy ways. It provides a focus and guidelines for their everyday interactions with children and helps them parent with confidence and consistency. And when children sense that parents know what they are doing, it adds to the youngsters' sense of security. ■

Family Situations

(A Closer Look at Behavior That Helps and Behavior That Hurts)

Family Situations

In interacting with children, how you do something is as important as what you do. The way we change an infant's diaper communicates much to the child about our level of caring and involvement. Offering children greater responsibility can make them feel important, but micro-managing the process and not giving any autonomy of action can make them feel unimportant and limit their learning possibilities. If a clear approach to childrearing is lacking, parent behavior is likely to be inconsistent. Actions and reactions between parents and children in different family situations frequently are based more on emotions than on reason.

In Chapter 1, many examples were presented of how inconsistent, reactive behavior interfered with satisfying the emotional needs of children and parents. In this chapter we will take a more detailed look at how this plays out in everyday life. Described below are actual situations gathered from conversations, interviews, seminars, and personal experiences. In each case, there is a discussion of what happened, how it might have been handled more effectively and its relation to the five critical needs of children.

SITUATION 1: RESPECT, ACCEPTANCE
(To Buy or Not To Buy?— A Shakespearean Dilemma)

A 10th grader, while shopping with her father in a book-store, discovered a large, costly book of Shakespeare's works and asked, "Dad, would you please buy this book for me?"

Dad, obviously annoyed, replied: "Are you kidding? That's just what you need, a big expensive book like that! With all the time you spend watching television, you'd probably never open it."

The child, looking hurt, replies meekly: "But, I'm doing well in school."

Behavior That Hurts

Rejecting the child's request in derogatory terms implies something the matter with her for expressing this desire. The child is showing interest in something educationally de-sirable. Even if it's unrealistic, superficial or just a whim, dismissing it out-of-hand cuts off communication. Dad's re-action is hurtful and provides little, if any, learning for his daughter.

Behavior That Helps

The following are suggested respectful and constructive alternative responses:

"It looks like a great book and Shakespeare is a wonderful writer, but it's expensive. Let's get one or two of his plays from the library, and after you have read them we'll buy something and start your own library. How does that sound?"

"How about if we get one of his plays and a biography from the library? We'll both read and discuss them and go from there. Ask your teacher to recommend which plays to read first."

Remarks

- ◆ Every interaction represents an opportunity to connect or disconnect with one's child.

- ◆ Here was a missed opportunity to try to connect with the child concerning education, money, and decision-making.

- ◆ We sometimes treat a child's expressed desire as though it were negative behavior.

- ◆ Accept a child's right to have unrealistic desires, even if you won't satisfy them.

- ◆ In rejecting a child's request, do so constructively, with love and respect.

- ◆ Negativity and sarcasm send the wrong message.

SITUATION 2: ACCEPTANCE, RESPECT
(Music Lover's Taste)

A teenage girl describes a conflict with her father as follows:

"Growing up in the sixties, my parents hated my music. I was constantly told to turn it down or turn it off. My father went so far as to institute a rule—for every hour of rock I listened to, I had to listen to one hour of classical music. It made me negative towards classical music."

Behavior That Hurts

The parents' hatred for the music, and objections to her listening to it, creates an adversarial relationship. Requiring her to listen to classical music under these conditions does not create interest, but rather turns the daughter off.

Behavior That Helps

To maintain positive relations, the father could express his own feelings about her music, but do so respectfully—his "holier than thou" attitude won't help. Regarding classical music, it would be more desirable and effective if the father would show his own interest and passion—let his daughter see the enthusiasm and positive feelings it evokes in him. Hopefully, her interest and curiosity would grow.

The father could invite her to listen with him to some recordings or attend a concert together. He could suggest a trade-off—he attends one of her events and she reciprocates.

Based on personal research or reading, he could also initiate a discussion with his daughter about the relationship between classical and rock music—this could be enlightening to both.

Remarks

+ Here was an opportunity for the parent to connect with the child concerning music.

+ Connecting is not possible if one party is inflexible, self-righteous or disrespectful towards another's taste.

+ Keeping an open mind can lead to mutual learning or at least to mutual tolerance.

• Accepting the daughter's right to her own taste in music increases the possibility of influencing her to expand her horizons.

• Selecting creative ways to stimulate another's interest is usually more productive than force-feeding.

SITUATION 3: INCLUSION, RESPECT, SECURITY (Parental Secrecy)

A 12-year-old boy describes his feelings of rejection as follows:

"One night I heard my mother and father in a loud argument in the other room. The next morning when I asked my mother what she and my father were arguing about, she replied, 'What goes on between me and your father is none of your business.' My concerns and feelings got smashed."

Behavior That Hurts

The mother's harshness in protecting her privacy is both unnecessary and harmful. The child's curiosity is crushed without the parent learning anything about the child's concerns. The mother's reaction might be displaced anger left over from the argument with her husband; it also might be the result of guilt or fear that her son might find out about a sensitive marital problem.

Behavior That Helps

The parent could have politely suggested that it was nothing her son needed to be concerned about, or that it was something she did not feel comfortable discussing at this time. She could have asked him why he was inquiring and then responded in a courteous and reassuring way. She might have decided to share some part of the argument of the night before in a limited or general way.

Remarks

+ As parents, we can profitably examine our fears, anxieties, and taboos which tend to restrict effectiveness with our children. Such a review might help us expand areas of inclusion for our children and handle areas of privacy more effectively.

+ Parents have a right to privacy, but when expressed with disdain it can have negative effects on the child.

+ Parents need to accept a child's right to be curious or concerned about what's going on with parents.

+ Sharing more with children, including concerns and problems, can reduce a child's anxieties and enhance feelings of belonging and security.

+ Listening to and sharing with children increases the probability that they will do the same with you.

SITUATION 4: RESPECT, IMPORTANCE
(My Room, My Castle)

A young adult describes one way his parents made him feel important as he was growing up:

"My mother and father said my room was my own and that's the way they treated it. They asked permission to enter, would never go through my things without first asking. I was in charge of how to decorate it—it changed as I did. I felt that it was truly my world and since it was respected, so was I."

Behavior That Hurts

The situation described above customarily is not the norm. In many cases, parents spend their children's teen years, and preteens too, nagging children about keeping their rooms clean—usually unsuccessfully. Typically, parents have not spelled out their expectations and the consequences for not meeting them. Even where they have been specified, these standards often change from week to week or moment to moment, with consequences deteriorating into idle threats. With consistent follow through lacking, the situation remains unresolved—the children annoyed by the constant harping and the parents frustrated by the lack of compliance.

Behavior That Helps

In the above situation, the parents apparently recognized the value in respecting their son's privacy and in giving him responsibility for making decisions about his living environment. They showed confidence in his ability to handle this responsibility and probably realized that he would benefit. It obviously contributed to his feelings of self-respect and importance.

Remarks

+ Giving children increasing degrees of responsibility—until or unless they prove themselves incapable of handling it—will help them become more responsible.

+ Too much control can limit the opportunity for development of a child's self-control.

+ Letting go of control is difficult for most parents. It means learning to live with anxiety and managing it.

♦ Parents should assess risk and introduce safeguards accordingly. This includes inspecting child's room when necessary.

♦ Parents should make a conscious effort to provide opportunities for children to grow in self-confidence.

**SITUATION 5: Respect, Security
(Grandma and Grandpa Know Best—
Or Do They?)**

One Saturday morning, Helen and Roger, her 8-year-old son, are visiting Marsha and George, Helen's mother and father-in-law. Roger is sitting on the floor leafing through a magazine when Marsha suddenly yells at her grandson in an impatient, angry tone: "Roger, put the magazine down and clear away your toys, this minute!" Roger says nothing and continues to look at the magazine.

Marsha gets up, walks over to Roger, rips the magazine out of his hand, pulls him by the collar over to the toys and says:

"Now put these away, right now! When I tell you to do something, do it immediately."

She then turns to Helen, and says, "Why don't you say something to him? Aren't you ever going to teach this kid some discipline? How can you allow him to be so disrespectful?"

Helen replies, "I don't think you should have yelled at him the way you did. Why didn't you just ask him in a nice way to pick up the toys?"

"Just wait, in a few years he'll be a teenager. Try to discipline him then, and he'll probably beat the hell out of you," shouts Marsha's husband angrily from across the living room.

According to Helen, Roger is generally a well-behaved child.

Behavior That Hurts

What is Marsha's goal in this situation? Is it to teach Roger good habits, discipline, or respect for elders? Expecting instantaneous and automatic compliance from Roger to her jarring demand is unrealistic and ineffective. Yelling and using physical force to impose her will seems exaggerated and counter-productive. Marsha's and George's hostility towards their daughter-in-law in front of her son poisons the atmosphere and creates an adversarial relationship. Roger can only be negatively affected by his grandmother's actions—either feeling guilty for having caused the situation or angry towards his grandparents because of the way they treated him and his mother.

Behavior That Helps

If the goal is to get the toys put away and for Roger to learn to take responsibility for doing so without being asked, the following are suggested approaches.

"Roger, would you do me a favor and put your magazine down for a minute and put your toys away. I'm afraid someone might trip over them."

"Roger, it would help me if you put things away when you are through with them. Then I wouldn't have to do it. I'd appreciate it."

Remarks

- To promote courteous, respectful behavior in children, treat them respectfully.

- Children want to please their parents. A consistent, respectful, positive approach will reinforce that desire.

 • When adult family members argue in front of their kids,
   and treat one another disrespectfully, the children's sense
   of security is threatened.

SITUATION 6: SECURITY, INCLUSION, ACCEPTANCE
(Parents' Divorce)

A 16-year old describes his feelings regarding his parents
divorce as follows:

"As my father and mother's relationship deteriorated to the
point of ending their 17-year-old marriage, I felt total
rejection. When my father moved out of the house I was
devastated. It was at that time I started to experiment with
drugs. I felt an incredible amount of anger and pain that
we couldn't stay together like other families—that my
father was going to start his life over while leaving ours all
screwed up."

Behavior That Hurts

Frequently parents do not realize that children feel personally rejected—even somehow to blame—when a divorce occurs; they may underestimate the negative effects of divorce
on children. Parents' expression of anger towards each other
adds to children's trauma. Discussions with the children are
often avoided because of feelings of fear, guilt, inadequacy,
and confusion.

Behavior That Helps

Ideally, a plan should be worked out and implemented
jointly by both parents which might include some of the
following:

1. Joint and individual discussions with the children to reassure them of your love and their lack of blame for the divorce.

2. To reduce fear of the unknown, provide children with details about those things that will change and how it will affect them.

3. Try not to overwhelm children with too much at one time. A family meeting with a counselor could be very helpful.

Remarks

* The negative effects on a child's sense of security caused by divorce can be long-lasting and powerful.

* Parents can reduce adverse effects of divorce on children by including them in discussions before, during, and after the process—also by setting aside animosities for the good of the children.

* Parents should not be surprised at a child's anger or resistance to discussions. Accept anger and continue to do your best at listening, understanding and reassuring.

SITUATION 7: ACCEPTANCE, INCLUSION, IMPORTANCE (Changing Baby's Diaper)

Anne had put her four-month-old Sarah on a table and abruptly started to change her diapers, with much resistance from the baby and lots of crying. The mother became increasingly more nervous and impatient with the baby. In a frustrated tone, the mother said such things as, "Now you stay still! You're going to get these diapers changed whether you like it or not." The child became increasingly upset as the mother's frustration increased.

The child's grandfather observed the interaction but didn't say anything until he got back to his home and telephoned his daughter. He gently suggested that his daughter might have reacted too impatiently and abruptly, that talking to the baby more, and not just handling her, might have helped.

The next day the young mother called her father and told him that his advice had made her day. She related that when the baby needed a change of diapers, she played with her first, then showed her two diapers, playfully encouraging her to make a choice, and proceeded to change her with no crying or fuss.

Behavior That Hurts

The baby's crying may have been a response to the abruptness of the change from play to diapers; this might have been especially true if the diaper change impetus came from a smell and not the baby's crying. The mother's nervousness and tone of voice exacerbated the discomfort already felt by the child from the bowel movement, and thus triggered the child's reaction. Being a first baby, the mother's inexperience was no doubt a factor.

Behavior That Helps

A four-month-old, doesn't have words or vocabulary to express desires, needs, satisfactions and frustrations. She relies on facial expressions, body movements, and sounds to convey her state of mind. A parent must be a patient, careful learner—listening and observing what the baby wants. A patient, playful attitude on the part of the parent is invaluable in having a calming and positive effect on the child.

Remarks

+ Babies are not objects; they have feelings about how we treat them.

+ Although babies can't speak, they do communicate. Parents need to be sensitive, aware listeners.

+ The goal should not only be to get the task done, but also to have a positive, playful interaction with the child.

+ Parents are not always fortunate enough to have someone observe the way they care for their child and who can provide constructive feedback. It is important for parents to become observers of their own behavior and to seek feedback from others.

+ Involving children in choices can contribute to their sense of importance and security, even at the earliest ages, and though they may not fully comprehend the alternatives. In this way, parents start practicing the art of inclusion early on.

SITUATION 8: ACCEPTANCE, SECURITY (To Let the Bird Fly or Not)

A happily married woman describes a tough choice that she and her parents made when she was 17:

"After some in-depth discussions, my parents gave me a choice to live at home or to move out and live with my older boyfriend. My parents and I had been in constant conflict about my staying overnight at his apartment several times a week and breaking other rules. They stated in very strong terms their preference for me to stay at home under the conditions which they spelled out, and said it would be very hard for them if I moved out. They stressed being tired of conflict, and if I stayed I would have to follow the rules. Once I made the decision, they allowed me to move out without recriminations."

Behavior That Hurts

Insisting that their daughter remain at home under the parent-imposed conditions was not working. Had the parents continued to insist, it probably would have led to further deterioration in their relations, with the daughter perhaps running away from home, and ending in a ruptured relationship.

Behavior That Helps

The parents put their fears and emotions aside in allowing their daughter to choose; they controlled their anxiety. The daughter spending evenings at the boyfriend's apartment resulted in ever-increasing tension, conflict and unhappiness at home. The parents decided that the status quo was unhealthy for the entire family which included two other siblings. They made sure the door was left open for the daughter to come back if the new situation did not work out.

Remarks

- Sometimes it's necessary to make the best out of a bad situation and choose between two alternatives, neither of which seems desirable.

- Giving a child responsibility for her own life, when it appears as a parent you cannot make the child do what you feel is right, is sometimes the best decision.

- Often the risks involved in a child's choice are not as dire as a parent imagines and can be reversed if things don't work.

- Accepting a decision with which the parent disagrees can enable the parent to maintain some influence in the long run.

• Including the child in decision-making enhances her sense of importance.

SITUATION 9: ACCEPTANCE, RESPECT, SECURITY (Forced Piano Playing)

How a father made a 9-year-old feel diminished is described as follows:

"I remember when my father made me feel like two cents because I didn't want to play the piano for guests at a Thanksgiving dinner at our house. He didn't ask me to play, he ordered me to. When I told him I didn't feel like it, he answered, 'What does that have to do with anything? Do you think I have the luxury of only doing things I feel like doing?' We got into an argument, with him calling me lazy and stubborn, which embarrassed me in front of the family."

Behavior That Hurts

The father fails to accept the child as an individual with feelings and needs of his own. He seems to look at his son's performance as a payoff for the money spent on lessons—"after all I've done for you" attitude. Parents often succumb to a common need to show off their children to others. The child's resistance becomes a challenge to parental authority and evokes their anger and disrespectful behavior towards the child.

Behavior That Helps

Parents need to think of how they would feel if someone in authority ordered them to perform; they need to recognize that children are not mechanical people who can be turned

on and off at will. Polite encouragement, with an escape
clause, would be more appropriate and effective: "Carl, I'd
love to have you play something for us, if you feel like it," or
"Would you like to play something for us? I'm sure everyone
would like to hear you."

Remarks

+ A child's security is threatened if expected to perform
  under any circumstances, on command, and without
  consent.

+ There are many situations like this where adults may
  succeed in forcing children to do something, but the
  amount of resentment and other unintended consequences can be costly.

+ Parents need to get their egos out of the way and accept
  a child's right to say "no" in areas that should be con-
  sensual.

+ Children are people too and can't be expected to always
  do what parents want them to do, on command.

+ Approaching children with courtesy and respect, order-
  ing less, requesting and encouraging more will pay off.

SITUATION 10: SECURITY, INCLUSION, IMPORTANCE
(Siblings Fighting/Parents' Despair)

Mary reports that her sons seem to be arguing and fighting with each other a lot, and it is driving her "nuts." She is
rarely consistent, and her general approach is to yell "stop it"
followed by threats of punishment which she occasionally
carries out. Sometimes she and her husband waste an inordinate amount of time trying to find out who started the

fight. Once in a while, one of the boys receives a spanking. Nothing seems to work. Mother and father sometimes argue in front of the kids about how to handle the current fight.

Behavior That Hurts

Since situations occur unexpectedly, parents generally react emotionally, out of frustration. They have no strategy regarding how to deal with them (e.g., what to ignore, what to address, how to respond in a more consistent manner, or how to prevent fights in the first place). Nagging, threatening and punishing become repetitious and lead to escalation of frustrations, with everyone feeling more insecure.

Behavior That Helps

Parents need to recognize that what they are doing isn't working, and that they must do something different. They need to make a distinction between prevention and remediation, brainstorm new ways to deal with each, and agree on approaches which both can support consistently.

For example, to emphasize prevention:

1. Make expectations and consequences clear to the children (e.g., arguing is acceptable, but hitting is unacceptable);

2. Have periodic family meetings to discuss such topics as why violence is unacceptable and alternative ways of handling frustrations;

3. Hold regular family feedback sessions giving children and parents an outlet, to talk out frustrations. (See Chapter 4, Game Plan #3)

Remarks

+ Not having a previously well-thought-out philosophy or strategy, parents often overreact, responding inconsistently in a mini-crisis atmosphere.

+ Emphasis needs to be on prevention rather than correction.

+ Include children in discussions of family values about aggressive behavior. This needs to begin early and be ongoing.

+ Include children in establishing clear behavioral expectations and consequences for deviations.

+ Expectations and consequences should be consistently adhered to and implemented with love and firmness, not anger.

+ When reasonable expectations and consequences are adhered to consistently by loving parents, children feel more secure.

+ Providing non-aggressive outlets for expression of family member's feelings and frustrations contributes to prevention.

+ Children should be praised when they work things out without fighting.

SITUATION 11: ACCEPTANCE, SECURITY
(Sex and the Pre-Teenager)

Six-year-old Kathy was dropped off by her mother at a neighbor's house early Saturday morning to spend a day with a school friend. Late that afternoon, Mom picked up Kathy and, on the way home, asked her if she had had fun with her friend. Kathy mentioned that one of the highlights was watching a wonderful movie on TV. When she told her mom the name of the movie, the latter was surprised, knowing that it contained sexually explicit language and scenes. Soon after, she was aghast when Kathy at one point, in telling the story of the movie, said, ". . . then I think he sexed her in the back seat of the car." The startled mom gasped, "Oh!" and quickly changed the subject. A moment of panic set in. Reflecting on it later, she vowed to screen more carefully what Kathy watched and whose home she could visit.

Behavior That Hurts

Parental fears often cause an overreaction to things that happen with children. In this case the mother was upset but did not act on her feelings. Some parents might have responded strongly, admonishing the child that she shouldn't watch things like that or talk about sex as she had—the implication being that she did something wrong.

Behavior That Helps

When surprised by a child's action, and not sure what to do, the best thing is to say nothing, which is what the mom did in this case. The parent can let it go and wait until the subject of sex comes up again, or until the child shows curiosity or initiates questions. On the other hand, recognizing the statement by Kathy to be ambiguous, the parent can initiate—in a low-key manner—exploration of where the child is at. For example, "When you say he sexed her in the back seat, what did you mean by that?" can provide an opportunity to find out what Kathy knows, how she feels about what she knows, and a chance to develop healthy attitudes about sex. Rather than a danger, here was an opportunity to connect with her daughter about sex.

Remarks

- ◆ For the child's sense of security and their own, parents need to have a strategy for dealing confidently with sensitive or taboo subjects such as sex, at a level appropriate to the child's maturity.

- ◆ If one accepts the notion of discussing sex with a child whenever the child raises the subject, or when the parent feels it may be timely, then parents need to be informed and prepared.

- ◆ Preparation will enable parents to take advantage of opportunities to connect with children confidently whenever the occasion presents itself.

SITUATION 12: INCLUSION
(A Failure to Communicate!)

Parents complain to friends about the difficulty of getting their 9- and 12-year-old children to communicate with them. The mother gives, as a typical example, the following interaction when one of them returns from school. Mother asks, "How was school today?" Child: "Okay." Mom: "What did you do?" Child: "Nothing." Mom: "Did you have fun?" Child: "No." Mom: "How come?" Child: "Boring."

Behavior That Hurts

The timing is poor. The child wants to change clothes and go out and play. The context for a real exchange is not favorable. The interaction is in an interview format, not an exchange. The child often feels that it is an interrogation. Questions are often mundane, and posed in an unenthusiastic manner, while the parent is doing something else. The exercise is more like a perfunctory ritual which sometimes takes place between husband and wife in marriages that have gone stale.

Behavior That Helps

Parents need to avoid squeezing in conversations on the run, or when a child's mind is elsewhere; selecting a favorable time for conversations is more likely to achieve a desired result. Initiating conversations where there is already initial interest would be helpful (e.g., a movie kids are talking about, something going on in the family or in the parent's own life, or a hot topic currently in the news).

Remarks

* Parents need to recognize and avoid repetitive, perfunctory, ritualistic conversations and talk about things of real interest.

* Set aside regular times for discussions (e.g., mealtimes, after dinner).

* Discuss things in your life that might be of interest to the children and events in their lives to stimulate conversation.

SITUATION 13: ACCEPTANCE, SECURITY
(Better Late Than Never—or Is It?)

A teenage son was out to a party with friends on a Saturday night. His mother had requested him to be home by midnight. He didn't get home until an hour later. When he arrived home, he started to apologize, but his mother interrupted, shouting that she had been "worried to death," that it was inexcusable he hadn't called to say he would be late, and that he would be punished. He protested angrily that he had tried to call, but that the line was busy. She accused him of lying.

He shouted back, "Stop treating me like a baby!" and stomped off to his room.

Behavior That Hurts

The mother's anger immediately put the boy on the defensive, and soon a conflict was underway, with each one matching the other's negative energy. She felt he was being thoughtless and insensitive to her concerns. He felt she was being hypocritical—if she had been "worried to death," why wasn't she happy or relieved to see him. Neither of them was able to see the situation from the other's viewpoint. Their emotions, and need to be right, kept them from a problem-solving approach; instead the situation escalated into a power struggle.

Behavior That Helps

Either one of them could have broken the cycle of matching each other's negative responses, and it could have been handled peacefully and agreeably. Ideally, the mother could have expressed her relief that he was okay and her concern caused by his not calling. She could have given him the benefit of the doubt about the phone call, hugged him and sent him to bed. The next day they could have discussed how to prevent the situation from happening again. The son could have ignored his mother's initial anger, and waited until she calmed down to apologize and discuss what happened.

Remarks

+ The parent's need for control and her anxiety come into conflict with the teenager's need for independence. Neither is able to think in terms of, "What can I do to help satisfy the other person's need, and possibly get what I want." Emotion takes over. The result is that no one benefits—neither peace of mind or control for the parent, nor independence for the son.

* Since such situations constantly reappear in different shapes and forms, parents need to develop a constructive strategy for avoiding and resolving problems.

* These interactions should be handled with mutual respect, seeking remedies rather than trying to establish blame or win an argument.

SUMMING UP

In most of the situations described above, we find interactions governed more by emotions than rationality. Differences escalate, leaving parents and children feeling stressed and unfulfilled. The emphasis is frequently on being right and forcing the other person to see it, not on understanding and satisfying one another's needs.

In the course of a year, most situations recur in varying degrees and forms. If we face each one as if we have never encountered it before, we will continue to shoot from the hip. However, if our approach is directed towards satisfying the child's five critical needs, we will be able to act more confidently, consistently, and positively—irrespective of the particular nature of each situation.

We can learn from each situation by using the critical needs as a guide in asking such questions as:

What would I have liked to have happen in the situation?

What did I learn about my own needs, behavior, strengths, weaknesses, thoughts, and attitudes?

With the five critical needs in mind, what could I have done differently?

By so doing, we will become better students of our own behavior and more conscious and effective parents. We will approach situations not as skirmishes to be won, but rather with the attitude that *every interaction with our children is an opportunity to teach and to learn, to connect or disconnect,* and with the intention of creating endless connections.

Recollections From Childhood

(Memories Have Impact)

*A*s children, we are very impressionable. Our parents have a great impact on us. For most of our childhood, our very survival depends on them. They're the ones with whom we spend the most time and are most intimately and emotionally involved. Since they become our main role models, for better or for worse, their influence on us is significant, often lasting far into our adult years and frequently affecting how we raise our own children.

At the time of a parent's death, you often hear people express regret that they had not gotten to know their parents better. Throughout our relatively brief lifespan more personal sharing between parent and child would appear desirable. Children are eager to know what parents think and feel, and why they do some of the things they do. Greater awareness of the effect of parent behavior on their children could contribute to more conscious and improved parenting.

In Chapter 2 we gave examples of supportive and non-supportive parent behavior in regard to the five critical needs of children. In this chapter, the children (teenagers through seniors) give first-hand recollections of their parents' behavior and how this affected whether or not they felt respected, important, accepted, included or secure during childhood.

The statements below represent a sample of responses to a questionnaire completed by over 200 individuals, most of them following a lecture or seminar on parent-child relations given by the author.

The task posed in the questionnaire was the following:

In thinking about your relationship with your parents, indicate on the attached questionnaire examples of communication, behavior, actions, attitudes of your parents which might possibly have affected—positively or negatively—your feeling respected, important, accepted, included, or secure as you were growing up.

Selected Responses

RESPECT

Not Feeling Respected

1. When I experimented with clothes, my folks made fun of me.

2. I was constantly interrupted before I could finish my thoughts.

3. When my mother took me shopping for clothes, she would end up shouting at me in public because I didn't like what she wanted to get me. I felt humiliated.

4. Sometimes I was embarrassed by comments that were made about me in my presence, as though I weren't there.

5. They showed me off, wanted me to be impressive to other people, never asked if it was okay with me. When I balked, they were upset and called me stubborn.

6. When I was little, my mother changed my pants outdoors after I spilled something. I was embarrassed.

7. When someone asked me a question, my mother or father would jump in and answer for me. It was very annoying.

Feeling Respected

1. My mother never opened my mail—she always respected my privacy.

2. When we misbehaved, our parents did not yell, or call us names.

3. If I didn't want to eat something, I was not forced to as long as I would try it.

4. My father did not like how some of my friends dressed, but they never stopped me from inviting them to our home.

5. My mom would apologize for losing her temper with me and sometimes explained what set her off.

6. When an uncle made fun of my long hair and referred to me as a girl, my mother asked him not to do that.

7. My parents didn't nag me about doing my homework. They just asked me to let them know when it was done.

IMPORTANCE

Not Feeling Important

1. It seemed I was frequently being told not to do something.

2. My father was an unhappy person. He would often tell me that I would never amount to anything. For a long time I believed him.

3. When my sister had emotional problems, my parents never discussed it with me. Because she was ill, she got most of the attention. All through my childhood, I felt she was important and I wasn't.

4. We were never part of decision making. For example, when we moved from Chicago to Tucson, my parents didn't ask our opinion or how we felt about changing schools.

5. When my mom got on the phone, my sister and I could not get her off to answer a question or talk to us; she was on the phone a lot.

6. When I placed second at a swim meet, my parents didn't seem enthusiastic and told me that I would have to work a lot harder to win. I was made to feel like a failure.

7. When I gave my opinion, my parents scornfully told me to keep quiet because I was too young to understand.

Feeling Important

1. They made time in their busy schedules to sit down and listen to me.

2. They occasionally shared with us what was going on in their lives.

3. Since I was a young child, I always worked in my father's office on weekends or vacation time. Although I started with simple tasks, I always felt very grownup to be allowed to spend time with my father in his world.

4. As an older sibling, my parents trusted me to watch over my sister as an early teen. They also allowed me to care for other young children and infants at an early age.

5. After my first semester at college, my parents let me prepare a budget for each semester. I had my own bank account and total control over all expenditures. They trusted that I would live within the budget and not confront them with emergencies.

6. My father worked at home as a cap-maker. I read articles to him from an adventure magazine while he worked. His enjoyment gave me a lot of pride and pleasure.

7. My parents gave me choices about clothes, food, friends, etc. When they didn't give me a choice, they explained why.

ACCEPTANCE

Not Feeling Accepted

1. When I displeased my mother, she'd say, "You're impossible. Why can't you be like your brother?"

2. When I decided I wanted to work after I finished school rather than go to college, I was made to feel like a failure.

3. I am 49 years old and my parents still criticize my decisions.

4. My parents always wanted to know about everything I was doing and were upset when I wouldn't tell them everything.

5. I felt as if my parents were always focusing on my faults. (My grandfather was an exception.)

6. Our parents never let us argue. They made us feel we were bad, rather than teach us how to argue.

7. Whenever I gave my father reasons for poor work in school, he would say he didn't want to hear excuses and wouldn't discuss it.

Feeling Accepted

1. My parents never objected to my inviting friends over, even when I didn't let them know in advance. Everyone was always welcome.

2. When I started to grow my hair long, I had a lot of trouble at school and with some of my relatives. My mom told me that it didn't really matter if my hair was long or short. It was what was inside a person that mattered.

3. I have always loved raw onions. No matter where we were, my mother always saw to it that I got raw onions with my hamburgers, hot dogs, corn flakes or whatever.

4. They didn't try to talk me out of my career goal even though they weren't enthusiastic about it.

5. I was acknowledged by my mother for my ability to relate to, and be patient with, my elderly grandparents.

6. They rarely interfered with my selection of friends and activities.

7. My parents didn't get upset when I expressed strong opinions about things with which they disagreed; instead, they discussed them with me.

INCLUSION

Not Feeling Included

1. When my sister went to a community center for psychotherapy, my mother and father went, but I was left out.

2. My family was famous for protecting us from the truth. There were a lot of skeletons in the closet, which eventually everyone knew about but couldn't discuss.

3. Our family did very little together.

4. I was never asked how I felt about important things or how I felt after a big family argument. I was never able to listen to my parents discuss anything significant.

5. When I was 10 years old my mother remarried, but she never discussed it with my brothers and me beforehand.

6. I was never included when parents had company; I was always sent to my room.

7. I felt excluded from my father's life. I wonder if he would have acted differently had I not been a girl.

Feeling Included

1. I always looked forward to holidays, family excursions, and family get-togethers.

2. There were often family discussions where decisions would be made. Everyone was included, and I was always asked my opinion.

3. My mother shared some secrets with me. Sometimes she would involve me in selecting a gift for my father and my name would be included on the card.

4. My father was a storyteller, and he would always oblige us when we asked for a "yarn." The stories were usually about his childhood and he shared how he felt in many different situations.

5. Every Sunday morning my parents would read the paper in bed. We used to climb into the bed and Dad would read us the comics, especially "Lil' Abner." It always ended with a "tickle-fight."

6. We did everything (well, almost everything) as a family. Every night during the work week, before going to sleep, we would play card games. My father would often play checkers with me and later, chess.

7. We did volunteer work together in community projects.

SECURITY

Not Feeling Secure

1. My parents' divorce was devastating, especially since they never discussed it adequately with us.

2. Constantly being criticized by my parents was unsettling.

3. My mother always seemed worried about money. Although we never discussed details, I felt we couldn't afford anything. I felt guilty every time I asked for anything.

4. Our parents fought a great deal, with a lot of anger; we didn't ever get to see them make up. It left a lasting mark on us.

5. Mom was out of the house a lot. We didn't feel she was around much.

6. My mom always said she was fat and ugly, so I thought I was too since people said I looked like her.

7. I was always afraid to talk to my parents about any troubles I had, because they would become very upset, and I did not receive the support I needed.

Feeling Secure

1. No matter how bad their finances were, my parents never complained and always seemed happy. Growing up, I felt sorry for the poor children who lived around us, and it wasn't until I was fully grown that I realized we were no better off financially than they were.

2. My mother always made me feel better when I was sick or when I was scared. Even when I got into trouble, I always felt secure because I knew she cared.

3. Someone was always at home when I was there—if not my parents, extended family members were around. I grew up in a very stable neighborhood.

4. One of my parents read to me every night when I went to bed, and they always began and ended each day with warm hugs.

5. My parents were divorced when I was seven. Neither of them let us feel less because of it. They never talked bad about each other and were always cordial in our presence. They explained what happened without laying blame—also made sure to emphasize that nothing was our fault.

6. My mother and father gave a lot to each other. I saw them as kind, tender, loving, very understanding, and deeply in love with each other. This was very reassuring.

7. Our parents never yelled or spanked us when we did something wrong; they'd take time to discuss it with us. Consequently, a disapproving look from either of our parents made a strong impression.

SUMMING UP

Parents are frequently unaware of the impact things they say or do have on their children. Years later, adults vividly remember the effect on them of certain aspects of their parents' behavior. Some of the things that affected children will surprise parents; many will recognize behavior as that of others, but not their own. Even when they recall their behavior, the negative effects may not be apparent to them. The level of parent consciousness needs to be raised in order for there to be a commitment to meeting the five critical needs of children.

As parents, we need to become students of our own behavior and regularly ask ourselves how we feel about our interactions with our children, what we have learned about ourselves, and what changes we need to make to become more effective, happier parents. We also need to ask our children questions to learn more about how we are impacting them. Children's fears and concerns often go unexpressed or misinterpreted. We need to share more of ourselves with our children, so they will learn how to share more with us, will want to share more, and will not fear to do so.

Becoming a
Professional at Parenting

(Childrearing Is
Too Important to
Leave to Chance)

*A*t a workshop for married couples, we met separately with husbands and wives. We asked the men what was the highest priority in their lives. Almost unanimously, the reply was, "My wife and children." We asked the wives how much time the husband spent with their children. The resounding consensus was something like, "We never see him. He's always doing something else." Sometimes our behavior does not match our stated priorities.

When we asked each group how much time they spent with their spouse in discussing how well they were doing as parents and in exploring ways in which they could improve, the answer to both was "almost none." Most of their conversations regarding childrearing occurred informally, when one of them didn't like something the other was doing or was upset or worried about something that was happening. Parenting collaboration for these couples was mostly problem- and crisis-oriented.

Amateur vs. Professional

Most parents are amateurs when it comes to parenting—that is, our behavior, both in quantity and in quality, belies the high priority we ascribe to childrearing. Our approach is hit or miss rather than systematic, reactive rather than proactive. There is nothing wrong with being an amateur. That's the way we all start out—untrained, inexperienced, unskilled—but hopefully with love in our hearts and a strong desire to learn and improve. The importance of parenting necessitates that we develop the expertise and systematic, conscious behavior of the professional, while conserving the love, enthusiasm and spontaneity of the amateur. Without the qualities of the amateur, the professional can become cold, mechanical, rigid; without the qualities of the professional, the amateur can become stumbling and ineffective.

Parenting is too important and complex to leave to chance. Given the goal of developing emotionally healthy children, a professional approach will increase the probability of doing so, and will additionally contribute to the emotional health of the parent. To remain amateurs means to continue a random approach which results in inconsistency, unnecessary stress, and frustration for both child and parent. As amateurs, some parents succeed better than others, but all are underachievers in regard to what they could accomplish.

Elements of Professionalism

Becoming more professional means possessing a set of core parenting values and applying them in a systematic and consistent way—translating concepts, ideas and intentions into action. The following discussion involves four essential elements of professionalism:

1. Making conscious decisions

2. Having a game plan

3. Becoming a student of one's own behavior

4. Having an experimental attitude

MAKING CONSCIOUS DECISIONS

The most consistent and predictable characteristic of contemporary society is change. Things are changing so rapidly that most of us are repeatedly brought up short by new circumstances. Pressures on families are strong. If parents do not focus on the family, children will be neglected.

Since change is inevitable, we have to decide whether to be a victim of forced change—that's what amateurs do—or become professionals and be part of planned change. Amateurs wait and let things happen. Professionals make conscious decisions and make things happen.

Planned change begins with a conscious decision by parents as to what they want their family life to be like. This is translated into goals and priorities which is the point of departure for developing plans.

HAVING A GAME PLAN

Without planning, a conscious decision or goal can be nothing but wishful thinking or lip service to a passing desire—like a New Year's resolution made on January 1st which is a distant memory by January 15th.

A game plan, very simply, is a statement of the actions to be taken to accomplish a goal. It can be simple or complex as required by the situation. A simple plan might be to keep a weekly anecdotal diary, recording progress towards meeting the child's five critical needs. Establishing a parent support group to meet on a regular basis would require more involved planning.

If you don't know where you are going, there's no telling where you'll wind up. If you know where you are going and have no plan to get there, you probably won't.

BECOMING A STUDENT OF YOUR OWN BEHAVIOR

Most of us are very good students of other people's behavior. We know exactly what others should do to make things better. Husbands know just how wives should change to make the marriage better; wives know the same regarding their husbands; children and parents could each give the other advice on what to do differently; equally so for employers and employees. And so it goes throughout society—if only other people would do things differently, the world and my life would be so much better.

Most of us are not very good students of our own behavior; rarely do we even consider this as a goal, let alone a priority. Yet we know it is very difficult, if not impossible, to change another's behavior. The one you have most control over is yourself, and changes in one's own behavior can have positive effects on others. Thus, in any relationship where the results are not what you would like, your point of departure must be that you, not the other person, must do something different. Common sense tells us why. If you are not getting what you want, then clearly whatever you have been doing to that point is not working. For example, if nagging and threatening for several years has not gotten your child to keep his room clean, then you need to do something different rather than to persist in ineffective, self-defeating behavior.

If we considered ourselves a corporation—John Doe, Inc.—wouldn't we want to periodically and regularly take stock of our assets and liabilities, our strengths and our weaknesses, and attempt to build on the strengths and overcome or correct the weaknesses? Otherwise, our weaknesses and liabilities could take over and cause us to go bankrupt. The high rate of divorce is an indication of how many marital relationships do go bankrupt, in which case the penalties paid by children are severe. As parents we are engaged in developing the most precious commodity of all, our children. Nowhere is there a greater need to become a student of one's own behavior than in parenting.

HAVING AN EXPERIMENTAL ATTITUDE

From one point of view, life is nothing but one big experiment, and all of society represents a wonderful laboratory for us to try things—especially regarding family life.

Recognizing this and consciously adopting an experimental attitude has many benefits. With an experimental attitude, there is no such thing as failure. You never let yourself become a victim. If something isn't working the way you want it to, you don't wring your hands and say, "Poor me! Why is this happening? What did I do to deserve this?" As an experimenter, you say "What am I going to try now to make it work?" You adhere to the cliché, "If at first you don't succeed, try, try again," but you add what most people omit "but each time in a different way." If you keep repeating something that isn't working, why would you expect the result to be different? In this case, practice does not make perfect. If you are practicing mistakes, you will get better and better at making mistakes. This is why many individuals do not become more effective at parenting through experience.

With an experimental attitude, problems and difficulties become challenges and daily living becomes a game, an experiment to have fun with. Each day affords the opportunity to use this wonderful laboratory, called *life*, to try something new. Parenting becomes a continuous, conscious experiment, a source of challenge and fascination to be savored.

Applying Elements of Professionalism

MAKING CONSCIOUS DECISIONS

When parents possess a clear set of core values, they are less likely to work at cross purposes or to misunderstand each other's actions or motives. It gives focus to their parenting activities and increases the probability that they will act more effectively and consistently.

The initial step in making the five critical needs of children an effective part of family life is to crystallize this intent with the following conscious decisions:

Adopting the Five Critical Needs

- ✦ I will adopt the five critical needs as core values to guide my behavior as follows:

  1. By treating my children with as much respect as I would want to receive, and as I try to give to adults.

  2. By treating my children in ways that enhance their feeling of being important, of having value.

  3. By accepting my children as unique, independent individuals entitled to their own ideas, feelings, thoughts, opinions.

  4. By helping my children feel a sense of community (a connection to others) by including them in family and community activities as much as possible.

  5. By increasing my children's feeling of security through role-modeling a loving, respectful relationship with my spouse, based on the five needs—or if a single parent, with the significant others in my life— and creating a balance between freedom and control.

Creating A Balanced Lifestyle

* Recognizing the benefits to my children of having re-laxed, happy parents who enjoy life, I will listen to my own needs as a person and engage in activities to satisfy them.

Becoming More Professional

* I will strive to become more professional at parenting through ongoing application of four basic elements—conscious decisions, game plan, student of own behavior, experimental attitude.

HAVING A GAME PLAN

Changing habits or starting new habits is not easy. Many good intentions break down because they never get converted to action. The suggested game plans presented below are designed to facilitate the transition from concept to action.

This is in no way a definitive list or a one-size-fits-all approach. It is presented to stimulate your thinking, to provide alternatives to choose from, adopt or modify. It is anticipated that you will create your own game plans appropriate to your particular situation, especially to the age, personalities, and needs of your family.

The idea is to make a commitment and get started immediately, even if only in a small way. Start with one game plan and build on this. It's better not to bite off too much and get started, than to wait until you can do it all and perhaps not do anything. As you gradually start doing things in a more systematic way, it will become easier and you will want to do more. Presented below are a variety of game plans for consideration.

GAME PLAN #1: Ongoing Review of Basic Concepts

Professional athletes and artists practice the basics of their field before each game or event—tennis players warm up before a match, practicing basic strokes; baseball players do infield and batting drills; musicians tune their instruments. Parents can't exactly replicate this behavior before meeting their children each day, but they can review the basic concepts of the five critical needs of children regularly as follows:

Goal

To keep the basic concepts of the five critical needs fresh as a daily guide to interactions with our children.

Actions

1. Weekly: Reread the *Summing Up* sections of Chapter 1 which summarize the rationale and importance of each of the five critical needs.

2. Quarterly: Reread the entire Chapter 1.

3. At the end of each week, parents should ask themselves if they need to review Chapter 1 more or less frequently.

Remarks

Eventually, with ongoing review and application, parents will solidify their mastery of the concepts and more easily reflect them in interactions with their children.

GAME PLAN #2: Becoming A Student of Your Own Behavior

Personal growth does not occur in a vacuum. We need to know how well we are doing—what's working and what's not—to make appropriate changes and adjustments. Professional athletes are fortunate in having objective data in the form of game and personal performance results, also the advantage of reviewing film, and feedback from coaches and trainers. It is difficult for parents to get similar objective feedback. Nevertheless, recognizing these limitations, parents can begin to become students of their own behavior through self-examination and requesting feedback from one's spouse, children, relatives and others.

Goal

To engage in activities that promote becoming a better student of one's own behavior.

Actions

1. Keep a daily journal by taking 15-20 minutes at the end of each day to reflect on the following questions:

    *   Did any of my actions help to satisfy any of my children's five critical needs? If yes, give brief examples.

    *   Did any of my actions today detract from satisfying any of the five needs? If yes, give brief examples.

    *   What did I learn about myself—attitudes, behavior, strengths, weaknesses?

    *   If I did today over, what would I change?

    *   Questions about my children's or my attitudes and behavior.

(See Appendix B for form to use in answering these questions.)

Remarks

Keeping such a journal—even for one month—will greatly surprise you as to how much you learn about yourself and your children, and how useful the information can be. An adjunct to this activity would be an end-of-week discussion by parents of content from their daily journals. This activity

alone can have a *profound* effect on the quality of the interactions with your child and your joy of parenting.

GAME PLAN #3: Family Feedback

Family feedback sessions, sometimes called family meetings, provide a forum for creating a safe, non-threatening
atmosphere for open communication to take place; they
provide an outlet for feelings, concerns, frustrations, appre-
ciations and joy. It is a sharing and learning situation where
everyone receives information about what's going on with
one another, and how one's actions might be affecting other
family members.

<u>Goal</u>

To Improve Family Relations Through Feedback Sessions.

<u>Actions</u>

1. Initial Meeting: Parents discuss purpose of meeting—
   i.e., to find out how everyone is doing so we can remove
   obstacles and make suggestions for leading happy,
   healthy lives together. Ground rules include: one person
   speaks at a time, no interruptions, everyone has equal
   permission to say anything.

2. Ongoing Weekly Sessions: the following open-ended
   questions are addressed in these sessions.

   ◆ What do we see one another doing that is getting in
     the way or helping us to lead happy, healthy lives?

   ◆ What do we like most and least about our family life?

   ◆ What else is going on in our lives that is causing us to
     feel good, bad, concerned, relaxed, appreciative?

   ◆ What could we be doing to make things better?

3. Parents set tone:

   ♦ Initially, parents may want to start sessions with a request for feedback—"What have I done this past week that you liked or didn't like?"

   ♦ To make it safe for children to respond honestly, parents need to be accepting of comments, and to emphasize that there will be no negative consequences for anything said.

   ♦ Some families begin with a round robin—each member takes 1-2 minutes to mention one's own highlights and lowlights for the past week, before engaging in feedback.

   ♦ Weekly: Following meetings take brief notes on any highlights of session.

   ♦ Monthly: Answer question—Do any theme(s) persist from week to week that appear to need more attention?

   (See Appendix C for form to use for above notes.)

Remarks

Giving and receiving honest feedback and open communication is not easy for most people; it may take a while for these sessions to become habitual, but gradually sessions will be easier and benefits will become obvious. You should not rush the process. Although talking about frustrations and offering criticism is part of feedback, some sessions may be devoted to things people feel good about. When matters come up that need problem-solving, follow-up can take place subsequently. Sessions may vary in frequency from weekly to once or twice a month, and in length from 30 minutes to one hour or more. Both frequency and length of sessions will depend on the needs of the family and may change over time. Family feedback sessions afford parents an opportunity to get to know and understand their children better, and children their parents.

GAME PLAN #4: Emphasizing Positive Reinforcement

Parents tend to pay more attention to kids when they misbehave than when they are doing things right. Kids are generally subject to much more criticism than praise; this can have a negative effect on their self-image and confidence. Children need more positive and less negative reinforcement.

Goal

To provide a child with numerous expressions of positive feedback daily.

Actions

Observe child's behavior with goal of acknowledging praiseworthy behavior. Praise should be for specific behavior appropriate to child's actions (e.g., not phony, or exaggerated).

Remarks

Through this activity, parents frequently discover more positive behavior than they might have expected. Parents should remember that praise must be sincere and deserved—"make-believe" will not work. One parent created a game with her son in which either one could initiate a positive interaction by saying, "I have a compliment for you when you have a compliment for me." When the second person is ready, the two exchange compliments. The reciprocal nature of this activity enables the child not only to experience the satisfaction of being acknowledged, but also of providing that pleasure for someone else.

GAME PLAN #5: Planning a Family Activity

Many parents engage in activities with children that are fun and interesting for the kids, but perhaps boring to the adults. Of course, the pleasure is in seeing the kids enjoying themselves or learning something. Parents will always be involved in a certain number of these activities. However, there are many activities the whole family can enjoy. When such activities accomplish a needed task, are fun for everyone, provide some learning, and give the kids a feeling of inclusion, you are accomplishing four things at once.

Goal

To create a family activity which promotes feelings of inclusion and importance for the children—garage sale/house uncluttering project.

Actions

1. Initial family meeting: Involve everyone in a meeting where the project is described and tasks, responsibilities, and income sharing are agreed upon, and completion dates for each activity described below are specified.

2. Making a list of things to sell: Each person independently makes a list of things to sell by answering the following questions:

   - What things of my own do I want to sell?

   - What are some things in the house that I don't like?

   - What are some things that nobody seems to use?

   - What are some things that I haven't worn or used in over a year?

   - What are some things I'm not sure I want to keep?

3. One or two persons are assigned to combine each person's selections into a master list, eliminating duplication.

4. Family meeting to arrive at a consensus on the final sale list.

5. Subsequent meeting(s) to plan the details of the sale—who does what, where, when, and how.

Remarks

The project does not have to be for conducting a garage sale. The purpose could be to unclutter the house, and items could be given to charity. Additional benefits might involve having children participate in delivering the items, and perhaps learning something about the receiving charity. A family party might be a fun conclusion to such a project. Other family activities/projects with similar goals could take place periodically.

In addition to feeling included and important, children learn planning, problem solving, conversation and teamwork skills.

GAME PLAN #6: Establishing Family Rules

Children feel more secure when they know what's expected of them, and where parent reactions are consistent and not subject to the whims or moods of either or both parents. When rules are well-thought-out and involve input from the children, they are more likely to be accepted.

Parents frequently avoid such discussions because they feel more comfortable exercising adult power. They are sometimes fearful of getting involved in endless debates where they might "give in to the kids." This again is operating out of fear. Yes, as kids grow older, they desire more power and independence, but parents should welcome this rather than fear it. Insecurity often leads to fear of losing control and the exercise of arbitrary power. In the end, however, this promotes endless conflict. Along with the desire for independence, kids have a strong need to please their parents and can be reasonable. Parents should help them by role-modeling rational discussion, decision making, compromise and cooperation.

Goal

To develop rules/guidelines of behavior for the family through the mechanism of shared planning and decision making.

Actions

1. Initial family meeting: Discuss the family unit as a microcosm of society in which mutual respect and cooperation are necessary for growth, happiness and security.

2. Follow-up meeting(s):

   + Briefly discuss (not all at one meeting) family values in relation to learning/education, health, work, interpersonal relations, etc.

   + Use family values as a context to discuss the need for rules—for schoolwork, homework, television, telephone, meals, bedtime, fighting, chores, etc. Seek consensus with children on rules and consequences when not adhered to.

   + Periodic meetings are held to monitor how things are going and to make changes where necessary.

Remarks

This activity can go a long way to eliminate emotional conflict and patterns of nagging, threats, punishment, frustration and submission. It should be stressed that the initial plan is the family's best thinking at the moment and that there will be ongoing evaluation. This activity can and should begin at an early age. To become skilled at participating in democratic environments and to appreciate their value, children need to experience them first hand, something which is not possible in autocratic schools and families. It should be made clear that every decision will not involve consensus-seeking, and in all cases, parents remain the final authority.

GAME PLAN #7: Creating Family Traditions

The breakdown of the American family—currently a worrisome concern permeating all segments of society—needs to be addressed by every parent.

Goal

To create events that combine elements of fun, interest, and learning that are repeated on a regular basis so as to become family traditions.

Actions

1. Parents discuss with children their intention to create special event evenings which would take place on a regular basis—frequency and time to be decided.

2. Family brainstorms ideas. For example:

   • Comedy evenings—each one brings in a joke to tell or a funny story to read.

   • Question and answer evenings, from a book such as Stock's *Book of Questions For Kids,* in which each person answers a question followed by family discussion. *(See Chapter 7 for a description of the book.)*

   • Being a student of your own behavior. Each family member states one thing from the previous day's behavior which he is not happy with and wishes to let go of; symbolically places it in a special bowl and rings a bell or chime; same thing is repeated for one thing individual feels good about and wishes to acknowledge self for. No comments by other family members.

◆ Gift-giving project—to encourage the concept that "it's better to give than to receive," or at least as important. Throughout the year, on occasions where people usually give gifts, involve the children in some way as a giver.

Remarks

Many families already engage in certain traditions. With some thought it should be easy to add to these. Many traditions continue throughout the children's growing-up years and sometimes beyond. *(See Appendix A for a list of over 150 potential family activities.)*

GAME PLAN #8: Family Reading/Storytelling Activity

One of the fond memories many people have of childhood is having parents read to them or tell them a story before going to bed. My father was a great storyteller, and it is something that became a ritual with me and my son. Each day would end with his getting into bed and my telling him a bedtime story and giving him a goodnight hug and kiss. This activity has become a tradition in many families, but not as many as one might hope. It is an excellent parent-child activity to end the day, providing comfort and pleasure to the child, along with motivation to read or improve learning skills. Also, it need not require much time or preparation and can be continued throughout childhood.

Goal

Establish reading as an important activity through a pleasurable and peaceful end-of-day parent-child interaction.

Actions

1. Start this activity as early as infancy, first with storytelling and then with reading from books. Librarians can recommend books that are popular at each age level.

2. Families with more than one child occasionally can have all participate at one time, with children taking turns reading or older ones reading to younger ones.

Remarks

At one elementary school in Los Angeles, the principal held a daily reading hour in order to emphasize the importance of reading. Everyone in the school—students, teachers, administrators, office and maintenance staff—stopped whatever they were doing and read for 45 minutes. This was followed by small group discussions. The interest level in this activity was high. As children get older, this can become a weekly family activity—perhaps from time to time everyone reading the same book.

GAME PLAN #9: A Team Approach to Cooking
and Kitchen Work

Parents can get more mileage out of projects by undertaking some which are immediately useful to the family, and also involve learning which is of lasting value. Kitchen activities around the preparation of meals offer such possibilities, especially since it is something that takes place several times each day.

Goal

To create a mini-culinary school which will provide children with gradually increasing responsibilities and skills.

Actions

1. Outline a brief curriculum for the gradual training of children in all tasks related to preparing and serving meals.

2. List tasks from simple to complex so as to be able to involve children at all ages (e.g., handing things to cook from refrigerator; setting table; opening cans; maintenance tasks such as cleaning table, putting things away, washing dishes, drying dishes, sweeping the floor; taking out the garbage; preparing vegetables; preparing simple snacks and meals such as hors d'oeuvres, cold sandwiches, cold and warm cereal, hard-boiled eggs, baked potatoes; making menu suggestions; preparing menus for different meals; serving guests; making a shopping list; assisting parent with shopping; doing shopping alone; simple and advanced cooking).

3. Assign tasks to children and titles according to responsibilities (e.g., assistant chef, maintenance chief).

4. Provide on-the-job instruction as necessary prior to performing each task.

Remarks

As children learn to do more and become more useful, it will contribute to their confidence and independence and help to lessen the parents' workload, which is especially important with single parent families or where both parents work. Parents who already have children perform some of the functions mentioned above can expand the activity.

GAME PLAN #10: Family Study of Meaning and
                        Significance of Respect

Children learn from role models. They can learn what to do and what not to do if they see enough of it, know what they are looking for, and can recognize and understand why something is positive or negative.

Goal

To create a deeper understanding of, and preference for, respectful behavior through active observation and discussion.

Actions

1. Parents discuss purpose of activity and define respectful and disrespectful behavior using examples from Chapter 1.

2. During a specified period (e.g., 1 week), each person makes notes of examples of disrespectful and respectful behavior at one or more of the following locations: at school, play, home, television. At the end of the week, the family meets to discuss results of observations and conclusions.

Remarks

This activity may be conducted at different intervals throughout the year. It provides another opportunity for parents to share their values with the children. From time to time, children and parents take note of their own acts of respect or disrespect and discuss them together.

GAME PLAN #11: Parent Self-Care

To create a positive, happy, relaxed family atmosphere, parents need to avoid the burnout pitfall—that is, being so involved in the care of their children that they neglect their own needs. When this happens, parents experience much stress, lack energy, feel less joy and are not as effective with their children. Parents need to nourish themselves as well as their children.

<u>Goal</u>

To identify activities that will satisfy parent's personal needs and prepare a plan to implement them.

<u>Actions</u>

1. Review areas of personal pursuits such as socializing, exercising, sports, travel, hobbies, learning, reading, volunteering, and so on, and identify those activities which would be high-priority choices.

2. Think about how much time you now spend in personal pursuits: alone, with your spouse or significant other, with friends. In each case, decide whether you want to spend the same, less, or more time in the future. *(See Appendix D for form to use for this survey.)*

3. With the information from 1 and 2 above, prepare a tentative plan for a period of time (e.g., 1, 3, 6, 12 months) to schedule the high-priority activities selected.

4. Weekly: Evaluate extent to which self-care plan is working. *(See Appendix E for form to use for this activity.)*

<u>Remarks</u>

Parents usually have a limited amount of time for personal pursuits. All the more reason to make conscious decisions about time alone, with your spouse, and with friends.

Since self-care is an area that parents many times neglect, having a plan adds focus and increases the probability of it occurring. As parents become better students of their own behavior, adjustments will be made to come up with a realistic, balanced approach.

GAME PLAN #12: Participating in a Parent Support Group

Parents can enlarge their vision of parenting and get practical support by discussing experiences with other parents, exchanging feedback, and supporting one another in numerous other ways.

Goal

To create a support group of parents interested in helping one another become more effective parents, with less stress, and more joy.

Actions

1. One or more parents invite others to a meeting to discuss the purpose, make-up, and procedures of such a group, and to establish a regular schedule for getting together.

2. Group can start with as few as two or three members and should not wait to recruit some arbitrary number of persons.

3. In addition to sharing ideas and experiences, other activities from which most parents can benefit include baby-sitting, sharing transportation, telephone hotline, trading children's clothing, loaning equipment, cooperative nursery, tutoring, exchanging books, etc.

Remarks

Parents who have participated in such groups have indicated that members become very close and frequently function like an extended family. Many have found that the group helped reduce stress and contributed to their becoming better parents.

Summing Up

The game plans in this chapter are not intended as an all-inclusive panacea. They are models which parents can adopt, modify or add to. Given the multiple demands and pressures on parents, we need to recognize that becoming a professional at parenting does not mean that everything has to be done at once.

It starts with the conscious decisions outlined at the beginning of this chapter which form the cornerstone of our approach to parenting. Here parents adopt, as core values, commitments to (1) meet the five critical needs of children, (2) seek to maintain a balanced lifestyle by not neglecting their own personal needs, and (3) achieve the foregoing by applying the four elements of professionalism. The basic components of the action strategy related to these commitments are contained in Game Plans #1, #2, #3, and #11. If parents implemented these four plans alone, it would have a strong, positive impact on children—and parents too!

Game Plan #1 provides for ongoing review of the five critical needs. In time it becomes second nature for these needs to guide parents in everyday interactions with their children. Game Plans #2 and #3 are specific tools for parents to become more aware of their own behavior and for the family to learn about its dynamics. In #2, parents keep a daily journal to identify what changes are needed to achieve positive results. In #3, the family meets as a whole to explore what is getting in their way or helping them to lead happy, productive lives. Game Plan #11 provides the framework for parents to attend to personal pursuits to fulfill themselves as parents and as persons. When the other game plans described in this chapter are added to the four discussed above, they represent activities for a lifetime of effective, joyful parenting.

In each case, parents have simple tools to assess how things are going and what needs to happen to make them better. Each parent continually asks the questions: "What have I learned about myself and my children?" "Is there anything that I need to do differently now?" The family collectively asks the same questions. Using Appendix F (Family Activities Survey) and Appendix G (Family Activities Evaluation), the family can prepare an overall plan for 3, 6, or 12 months.

Appendices B and C provide a daily and weekly procedure for parents to note (1) any areas of concern about their children and (2) any questions they have about the children's, or their own, attitudes and behavior. Appendix H, Children's Well-Being Survey, provides parents an opportunity to assess how well their children are progressing with their lives. Each spouse can complete it separately (weekly or monthly) and discuss their observations. If any concerns or questions occur, parents can plan some action or decide to seek information from the varied sources available (e.g., books, other parents, teachers, school counselors, child psychologists, and other mental health professionals).

With these tools, they become conscious of what is and is not happening in the family. It also is something tangible to help maintain their awareness.

In addition to satisfying children's five critical needs and strengthening family cohesion, potential by-products from these activities include improving children's reading, writing, problem-solving and other skills, both cognitive and affective. They also provide opportunities for fun, relaxation, challenge, adventure, and experimentation, offering possibilities for significant enrichment of family life.

Individuals, like organizations, must continually be able to adapt to change and renew themselves. This is particularly true in contemporary society, and for the foreseeable future, where the most constant and predictable characteristic is change. A strategy for self-renewal and self-correction helps us to confront change and adapt to new conditions. Applying the four elements of professionalism—making conscious decisions, having a game plan, being a student of your own behavior, having an experimental attitude—provides a framework for parents to satisfy children's five critical needs and strengthen family cohesion in a positive, consistent, and efficient manner. ∎

F I V E

Overcoming Obstacles
and Taking Control

*(Maintaining Focus and a
Balanced Lifestyle)*

*T*he process of becoming more professional at parenting will not be without difficulties. With this in mind, it is worth revisiting, with greater focus, certain themes previously addressed. The intention is to anticipate and be better prepared to overcome or avoid certain obstacles and pitfalls which you are sure to face.

Obstacles

FEELING OVERWHELMED

A common problem that parents often emphasize is stress—that is, having feelings of being overwhelmed, of having too much to do, of being frustrated or worn out. The question frequently asked, with an overtone of helplessness, is: "Where do I find the time to do everything I have to do?" As one mother said, "How can I implement all these wonderful ideas when I can't even find time to prepare a proper meal or do the laundry." When both parents work, or in the case of a single parent, the problems are further exacerbated.

In addition to the actual amount of work involved in parenting, a considerable amount of energy often goes into worry. Golda Meier, former prime minister of Israel, wrote in her autobiography about the worry, guilt and stress she experienced because of the conflicting demands of work and family. When at work she worried about the kids, when at home she worried about her work. In such situations, some amount of worry is inevitable. However, it is not in our own or our children's best interest to become overwhelmed by such worry.

NEGLECT OF PLANNING

Common sense tells us that when you have more to do than time available, something must give. What gets neglected should not be left to chance. It should be a conscious decision. Short of this, you will continue to feel overwhelmed because of all the things you didn't get done, even though there was no way to have done them in the first place. Sometimes the kids are victims of this neglect, other times it is the parents, but in either case it is the family as a whole that suffers.

RESISTANCE TO PLANNING

The situation described above calls for planning—establishing priorities, assigning responsibilities, allocating time, simplifying one's life, making conscious choices. This type of planning is not rocket science—effective parents do it intuitively—but all too often, it does not happen. Some of the reasons for this are described below.

Cultural Conditioning

Our culture generally values *doing* rather than *thinking* or *planning*. As a consultant to schools and corporations, I would often hear an administrator or executive at a planning meeting state that the meeting should be cut short so everyone could get back to work. Planning was not considered work. One can understand that planning isn't as rewarding as doing something where you see immediate results for your efforts. However, the truth is that the busier you are, the more carefully you have to plan—although it takes time, it saves much more. Nevertheless, as one parent said, "I don't have time to plan. I'm too far behind already."

Myth of Spontaneity

There is also what I like to call *the myth of spontaneity*. Some people feel constrained by a plan or a schedule. They place a high value on being spontaneous and feel locked in by structure. But without a plan, they tend to react to whatever comes up at the moment and not according to any priority. Consequently, important things are sometimes neglected and lesser ones get done. Consistency, which is so important to children, is sacrificed. The purpose of planning is to insure that the things we say are important actually do occur, and in a timely and consistent manner.

Planning in no way interferes with spontaneity, inspiration or intuition. If anything occurs that evokes a desire to deviate, we should remember it is our plan and we can do what we want. In fact, having a plan facilitates spontaneity, since we have the security of a basic structure to return to.

The famous Russian theater director, Stanislavski, once cautioned actors that since inspiration occurred so rarely, it was essential to master the basics. This underlines a misconception about how artists and other creative people work—far from being undisciplined, they are among the most disciplined persons we know. When someone once asked a very successful composer when he composed, he replied, "From nine to five."

Advantages of Being Overwhelmed

As much as we may protest and complain about being overwhelmed, I believe that many of us unconsciously keep ourselves in this position because of hidden benefits. For one thing, it enables a parent to feel like a martyr and to evoke sympathy. People are less likely to place demands on us if we are overwhelmed. It makes us less accountable when we make mistakes or forget to do something. After all, what can anyone expect, given how overwhelmed we are. Sometimes, because of this, we unconsciously subvert our own efforts to plan, to get organized, to make things work.

OVER-SERIOUSNESS

We parents tend to take everything too seriously, especially ourselves. This tendency probably reaches its height with the arrival of our first child, but does not ever completely go away. We agonize over decisions as though our child's life depended on each one. We are sometimes conscientious to a fault. If things are going okay today, we'll worry about tomorrow. If we could, we would live our children's lives for them attempting to spare them any suffering or pain. In the process, we create a heavy atmosphere and sometimes become a burden to ourselves and to our children.

We need to lighten up, cut the drama and move to joy—creating a family atmosphere filled with laughter, enjoyment and some of the sheer silliness of daily living. Sometimes we forget about the beneficial effects of laughter, how it strengthens the immune system, combats illness, and contributes an upbeat tone to the quality of our lives.

Children are very funny, and we adults are downright comical at times too. We can do our children and ourselves a great favor by promoting and indulging in laughter at home and by not taking ourselves so seriously. Kids think it's great fun when their parents laugh, especially when they are able to laugh at themselves.

UNREALISTIC EXPECTATIONS

As we make changes or try to do something new, we sometimes become discouraged or disappointed when things do not run smoothly or positive results are not achieved immediately. We should know from experience that the real world doesn't work that way. This can be especially frustrating when we have made plans involving the whole family, and at the last minute one of the children refuses to participate, or a change in a family routine meets with strong resistance, or a child acts out in some way and a family conflict erupts. These are not times to lose heart.

Families, like groups, organizations, cities and nations start and stop, miss a few times and then start over again. When the word *regular* is used in conjunction with a proposed activity or game plan, we must recognize that it simply won't happen every time. At times, the solution to one problem will create another. And at other times, it may appear that nothing is working.

We need to be committed to the notion that a philosophy, a strategy or a good idea is not to be abandoned simply because of obstacles or mistakes. These come with the territory.

Taking Control of Your Life

So, what's a parent to do? How do you get everything done in the limited time available? The answer is to take control of your life. Recognize that some of the pressures you feel are self-imposed and unnecessary. Begin by getting rid of these. Remind yourself that no matter how much you have to do or how limited your resources, there are always choices to be made and by making them, stress can be reduced substantially. However, you must be ready to let go of being overwhelmed. Some parents are always overwhelmed; others are underwhelmed. The goal here is to get everyone just "whelmed."

Becoming a professional at parenting means becoming a more conscious parent. It means recognizing that if you feel overwhelmed, it's an indication that you are doing too much and/or behaving inefficiently. Most likely you are not making choices—sometimes difficult ones. The following are suggestions to help you move towards taking better control of your life.

PREPARE PRELIMINARY TO-DO LIST

Carrying in your head the details of everything you have to or want to do is both a strain and inefficient. The first step in taking control of your life is to make a written list of everything you believe (or imagine) you have to do in the next 90 days—brainstorm this list, doing it rather quickly without dwelling on any item. If a glance at your rough list indicates that there is more to do than time available—which is usually the case—rethink your situation and eliminate any item that you feel is not essential. If you might want to do it eventually, place it on a "future" list.

PRIORITIZE AND SCHEDULE

At this stage, you need to make conscious decisions as to which activities/tasks are most important so that they don't get overlooked, neglected, or short-changed. Select things you feel must be done in the next 30 days.

Using your knowledge of the family situation, your own behavior, and the activities involved, prepare a 30-day calendar allocating specific days and time blocks for each activity. This is your conscious thinking as to the most practical days and time of day to get things done efficiently.

By creating a written plan, you will frequently find there is not enough time to achieve everything you had in mind. In this case, you must either create additional time or eliminate something from the schedule.

CREATING ADDITIONAL TIME

+ *Extend the work day.*
  Unfortunately, many parents try to sleep fewer hours by going to sleep later and/or getting up earlier. This is not recommended. It's what leads to being overwhelmed—better to select one or more of the suggestions described below.

+ *Create more time by simplifying various aspects of your life and by managing your time more efficiently.*
  Follow anyone around for an entire day and you would find a considerable amount of inefficient use of time, much more than most of us realize. This can contribute significantly to our feelings of being stressed out. A few examples are:

  – Too many trips for errands which could be combined

  – Procrastination

- Unnecessary phone calls and/or long phone calls

- Not preparing things for the next day

- Agreeing to do something which you really didn't want or need to do

- Not concentrating on one thing at a time, and accumulating a backlog of unfinished tasks

- Not setting priorities

- Too many distractions

* *Do some things less thoroughly or less frequently.*
  Not everything has to be done with the same thoroughness or frequency. You can have a family activity every other week rather than every week, do a major house cleaning once a month rather than weekly, shop for food only once a week, and so forth.

* *Delegate.*
  Get help from your spouse, children, and extended family (grandparents, siblings, other relatives). Parenting is a full-time responsibility, but parents are not the only ones who can be caregivers and household helpers. Sharing household responsibilities with children has multiple benefits. In addition to lessening the pressure on parents, it provides an opportunity for children to acquire some skills and to feel important. Extended family can help with baby-sitting, tutoring, and much more.

* *Barter.*
  Exchange help with someone (e.g., look after a neighbor's children along with your own and have them do the same for you).

- *Pay for help.*
  Where economically feasible, pay someone to handle
  certain tasks to reduce workload and/or provide free
  time. Even where money is a problem, sacrificing something material for household or childcare help is a trade-
  off worth considering.

- *Networking.*
  Create or join a support group where parents help one
  another with certain tasks on a rotating basis and support
  one another in many different ways.

- *Reduce unnecessary worry.*
  Cut down on the amount of psychic energy that goes into
  unnecessary worrying about your child. Yes, the world is
  a dangerous place and there are many things to be
  concerned about. On the other hand, you can make
  yourself miserable 24 hours a day with unproductive and
  unrealistic worrying. It can help to reduce some of this
  worry by distinguishing between low- and high-risk activities, and by recognizing that because something is
  possible doesn't mean it is probable. Concentrate your
  efforts on the high-risk, high-probability areas. Minimize
  or eliminate concern in the low-risk, low-probability
  realm.

- *Reduce negative effects of false emergencies, interruptions, and distractions.*
  Some interruptions and distractions occur because of our
  lack of discipline. With resolve these can be eliminated.
  Some emergencies and interruptions cannot be avoided
  and must be handled without delay. Other ones are not
  real and should not require an immediate response.
  Parents need to be able to discern the one from the other.

(For an abundance of additional time-saving ideas, Chapter 7 contains descriptions of two excellent books, Kathy Peel's *The Family Manager's Guide for Working Moms,* and Elaine St. James', *Simplify Your Life with Kids.*)

ONGOING PLANNING AND REVISION

Given the possibilities described above to parent smarter rather than harder, you are in a position to (a) prepare a plan that is more realistic, less stressful, and more productive, and (b) evaluate results and make adjustments along the way. Evaluation of the schedule involves looking at what was actually done as related to what was planned, and deciding what, if anything, needs to change. The longer you stay with the process, the more skilled you become and the easier it gets.

Summing Up

There always will be conflicts between the things that you need to get done for your family, your career, and your own personal nurturing. You will never be able to do everything. Time is limited and tasks to be performed are unlimited, but you can only do what you can do. Having a framework for making conscious decisions about trade-offs, compromises and adjustments will ease the task; yet it will not be easy. It will require discipline, practice, and perseverance, but it is worth the effort. After all, if it doesn't work, you can always go back to being overwhelmed!

A final thought—no matter how good you get at taking control of your life, there always will be moments of feeling overwhelmed. At these times, you might well consider the following advice suggested to me by a mother: "When all hell seems to be breaking loose, and I am feeling overwhelmed— there are dishes in the sink, dinner hasn't been prepared, shopping needs to be done, the house is a mess, the baby is crying, my back is hurting, and I feel like screaming—I've learned to stop, take a deep breath, and ask myself, 'What's the most important thing I can do right now?' Then I pick up my baby, sit down with her on my lap in the living room, take the phone off the hook and do nothing for a while. It's amazing how things seem to fall into place after that."

Implications for Families and Schools

(Creating and Extending a Sense of Community)

Families

A SENSE OF COMMUNITY

Ideally, families would function as a team in the best tradition of the word, as in: *team effort*—everyone pulls together for the good of the whole; *team play*—collective play with mutual assistance of members; *teamwork*—several associates each doing a part, subordinating personal prominence to the efficiency of the whole. In practice, however, some families seem closer to another definition, *team*—two or more draft animals harnessed to the same vehicle.

A speaker at a national conference on education once said, "The problem with many of our cities is that they are encampments of strangers and not communities." This is also a problem with many families. Too often in our modern, complex, fast moving, high-tech societies, families do not always develop a sense of community and children get lost in the rush. To create this sense of community, families need to be involved with one another, to do things together.

Families that do things together create camaraderie, cohesion. Families that do things together that are fun and interesting create a positive atmosphere. Families that do things together that encourage members to think, ask questions and express themselves become learning communities. Families that do things together on a regular basis create traditions. Families that create traditions develop a strong sense of community, displaying mutual respect, caring, and support. The children of families with a strong sense of community are more resistant to outside negative influences, more likely to be influenced by positive role models within the family, and to become emotionally healthy citizens at home, in school, and within society at large.

Core Values

The strength of the family emanates from parents and their convictions. If there is no coherent philosophy, strategy or approach to childrearing, and if values are not clear, parent behavior can be inconsistent and confusing. It behooves parents to define values for themselves and to emphasize them in the family. If we think of family values as values shared by all members of the family, it becomes something very much worth striving for.

Adopting the five critical needs as an integral component of a family's core values provides a valuable framework to guide parents' interactions with their children and to evaluate their parenting effectiveness. Additionally, it does much more. As parents treat each other in ways that satisfy the five needs, they become role models for the kids on how to act in a loving way. Further, as parents communicate to children that they have the same needs and express positive feelings at the children's behavior that satisfy these needs, they begin to become true family values. Children are stimulated to start thinking not only about what's being done and not done to, for, and with them, but also about how their behavior impacts others.

Since the five needs represent a concept that can be applied to all interactions and transactions among individuals, the children's and parents' understanding and appreciation of them are certain to grow over time. Children can learn about the power of their behavior to impact positively not only each other and their parents, but also relatives, friends, teachers, acquaintances—almost anyone with whom they have contact. This not only helps to strengthen a sense of community among family members, but also reaches out to encompass more of society and give children a larger view of *community.*

Self-Sacrifice/Self-Care

Most everyone would agree that parenting involves sacrifice and self-denial. However, there is a point where both can be overdone to the detriment of parent and child. If we become so obsessed with our responsibilities as parents that we are tense, exhausted or irritable a lot of the time, we will be harming ourselves, our children and probably our marriage. It is not necessary to be doing something for and with our children all the time; providing some *alone time* for kids to manage themselves—for their own amusement, interest, exploration, and discovery—can be a significant part of their growth. Often, what impacts children strongly about their childhood is whether the home was a pleasant, relaxed place— where mom and dad were fun to be around, rather than a family atmosphere filled with tension, worry, and confusion.

As important as it is to nurture our children, it is equally necessary to nurture ourselves as human beings; the two are closely related. Yes, parents need to sacrifice for their children, but this should not mean giving up all personal goals or desires. We need to learn how to sacrifice, without sacrificing ourselves. For some, this might mean staying at home full time; for others it will involve a part or full-time career. For all parents, it must include finding some time for personal pursuits such as social contacts, travel, sports, exercise, reading, solitude, volunteering, charity work—without feeling guilty. It is healthy for parents and for kids to have time by themselves.

Making It Happen

As we well know, having lofty ideas and convictions alone will not make it happen. We must be able to translate them into action. Since most parents find that they usually have more to do than time available, it is easy to direct energy to where the pressure appears the greatest or where our inclinations and gratifications are the strongest. If time is not specifically allocated to family activities, it will most certainly be absorbed elsewhere—parenting will be business as usual, catch-as-catch-can.

Another core value has to do with making it happen—to the need for a conscious decision, a commitment to achieving a strong sense of community within the family—and not leaving it to chance. Planning gets us away from a crisis-oriented mode of correcting, threatening, disciplining and punishing children. It changes the focus to creating a positive family atmosphere with an emphasis on mutually satisfying activities.

Parents consciously need to seek as much balance as possible between career and home, work and play, time together and time alone in order to achieve an emotionally healthy family with a strong sense of community.

FIRST FIVE YEARS OF LIFE

Many new parents are so excited and filled with joy at the birth of their child that the complexity and enormity of parenting doesn't hit them right away. Soon, however, they begin to face the realities of 24 hours a day of constant responsibility and caring for the newborn.

In preparing for the act of giving birth, parents sometimes spend months during pregnancy in classes, discussion groups and reading, and this time is well spent. Parents learn about some of the difficulties they will face and take steps to avoid them through diet, physical conditioning and relaxation exercises. Preparation for meeting the child's five critical needs should also begin during pregnancy, and behavior to meet these emotional needs should begin at birth.

Given the general agreement among experts as to the importance of the early years of life in the healthy development of children, getting them off to the best possible start should be primary in our thinking.

From the _I Am Your Child_ campaign, founded by Michele and Rob Reiner, two resources especially helpful to new parents are _The First Years Last Forever_ parenting booklet (free) and _The First Years Last Forever_ video ($5)—both can be ordered in English or Spanish by calling 1-888-447-3400.

TEENAGERS

Adopting the five critical needs and a professional approach to parenting early in a child's life will go a long way to reducing problems parents experience when children become teenagers. However, even when this approach is started late, there are benefits to be derived.

Teenagers can come to recognize that parents are not their adversaries—that every night just before they go to sleep, parents do not make up a list entitled, "How Many Ways Can I Make My Child Miserable Tomorrow." On the contrary, children can learn that parents have the same five critical needs as they do. And that sometimes, although parents generally try to act with a child's best interest in mind, they are not perfect and don't always make the right decision.

Understanding and accepting that parents are fallible, teenagers can learn that differences and conflicts can best be resolved through discussion, compromise—and yes, sometimes acceptance of parental authority—rather than through tantrums, acting-out, name-calling and put-downs by either parent or child.

Children can learn that by assisting parents in meeting their needs they can get along better and get more of what they want. For example, understanding the parents' need to feel secure about their safety, they will recognize that it won't help to say, "I promise you I won't have an accident." That would not be reassuring, nor would it likely get them the permission they seek. Specifying the steps they intend to take to insure safety and soliciting suggestions from their parents would be much more effective.

Parents have the responsibility for communicating their needs so that teenagers can hear and understand them, and not have to decipher mixed messages. Teenagers feel more secure when they observe that mom and dad are on the same wave length regarding childrearing, and are committed to treating each other and the kids in ways that satisfy the five critical needs. Equally important is parents sharing more of their feelings and values directly with children, and making their desires clear as to how they expect to be treated.

For all children, not just teenagers, one of the goals and anticipated outcomes of growing up in a positive family atmosphere, where the mutuality of meeting one another's needs is emphasized, is movement away from self-centeredness. Children will learn the importance and value of interacting with their parents, siblings, and others in ways that contribute to satisfying everyone's major emotional needs.

SIGNIFICANT OTHERS

Of concern to parents is getting significant others who interact with their children—grandparents, teachers, child care agencies, hospitals and baby-sitters—to relate to the youngsters in ways that support the parents' goals. Parents can use their core philosophy as a guideline to observe these individuals and institutions, and make suggestions to help them better meet family needs.

SINGLE-PARENT FAMILIES

Much of what we have described in this book applies equally to single-parent families. In many ways, it is even more important for the single parent to have this core philosophy of the five critical needs as a foundation for parenting. Given the pressures on these parents, this would provide a structure for more positive and consistent interactions with the children. Also, networking with other parents (e.g., joining a parent support group as described in Chapter 4, Game Plan #12) would be highly desirable.

PARENTS IN SECOND MARRIAGES

With the high divorce rate and subsequent large numbers of remarriages, step-parenting becomes an important consideration. Many stepparents and stepchildren find the situation uncomfortable and difficult. Living with someone else's children can be awkward and frustrating, adding to the normal stresses of a second marriage. Here, the structure of game plans, as described in Chapter 4, can offer the stepparents a more comfortable and effective way to create positive relations with their spouse's children. (See Chapter 7 for a description of an informative book on this subject by Jeannette

Lofas, *Stepparenting: Everything You Need to Know to Make It Work!*)

SUMMING UP

Currently, there is much talk in society about family values and having a sense of community. Everyone seems to agree about the importance of family values, but frequently interpret the details differently. For example, the media depicts a certain family situation, and this is followed by a polemic as to whether it was pro- or anti-family values. Sometimes we listen to the debate on the radio, watch it on TV or read about it in the newspapers—but more as spectators than as participants.

Creating a strong family and sense of community, however, is not a spectator sport. Whether you are part of a traditional or non-traditional, two-parent family, or a single-parent or stepparent situation, you will need to have a clear vision of what you want your family life to be and a committed approach to achieving it. In essence, it requires direction, time and effort—that's how you are likely to get results. Time and activities with children must not be left to chance. Planning can insure quality and quantity.

At the same time, parents must take care of themselves and schedule time for satisfying activities alone and as a couple. The need to create a positive, relaxed atmosphere in which fun and laughter play an important role cannot be over-emphasized. One of the most important things we can do for our children is to surround them with parents who are relaxed and enjoying life. Parents have the power to make childrearing less stressful, more positive, and more pleasurable. It is essential for their own and their children's well-being that they do so.

Family as a Learning Community

As parents and children become better students of their own behavior, they are able to help one another recognize when they are relating in emotionally healthy or unhealthy ways. This is the beginning of the family as a *learning community*. As such, it is no longer business as usual with parents as paragons of knowledge and virtue to be passed on to their kids so they can become just like their moms and dads. It recognizes that adults are not finished products but rather *adults in training*—imperfect, fallible human beings. Family members understand that *all of them* need to learn how to become better persons, and that this learning can occur as a family—children from parents, parents from children, and all together. As part of this process, parents may want to have their teenagers (and where appropriate pre-teens too) read this book and discuss it together—chapter by chapter, situation by situation, and game plan by game plan. Such a discussion with its accompanying personal sharing, could further their getting to know one another better as people and not just in the roles of mother, father, and child.

Schools

Next to the family, the schools have perhaps the greatest influence in meeting the five critical needs of children. Yet, the schools have as many or more problems than the beleaguered family.

The public school crises and the anguished cries for reform of the '60s, '70s, and '80s have moved on to the '90s. Only now the crises appear greater, the anguished cries louder, and the demands for reform more urgent. The problems of low achievement, inadequate financing, declining student and teacher morale, and poor school/parent relations continue unabated. At the same time, the dissatisfaction voiced by almost everyone—students, parents, teachers, school districts and schools, business community, and government—is accompanied by increasingly stronger demands for change.

SCHOOLS AND THE FIVE CRITICAL NEEDS

The need for cost-effective educational models that offer constructive, positive changes that are fundamental and systemic rather than cosmetic, has never been greater. Because of the diversity of schools and the changing emotional climate, models are needed that cut across geographical, ethnic, and socio-economic boundaries. They must create in all the principal participants a proprietary interest in the school.

This author was co-director of a Ford Foundation sponsored project which created such a model school at the elementary level (grades K-6) in the Los Angeles city schools in the 1970s. In this new school children, parents, teachers, community members, and administrators shared responsibility, accountability, and authority and were empowered to revitalize the educational process.

Four major concepts were the guiding force of the schools: shared learning/teaching (all students became teachers of other students as a central instructional method), shared planning and decision making (students, parents, teachers, and administrators participated actively in governing the school), shared feedback and accountability (a self-correcting mechanism enabling the school and all participants to become students of their own behavior), and parent/community involvement (parents involved in all aspects of school and the community itself became a classroom for the school). It is a cost-effective program that draws on and maximizes the resources already available in each school and community—the people themselves.

It's easy to see how such a school promotes the five critical needs of children and why I like to call it a *community of big shots*(i.e., everyone is included, accepted, feels important, and the atmosphere is one of mutual respect). It represents a learning community where everyone cares about, and becomes involved in, the well-being of everyone else. (The concept of extending this program to secondary education is discussed in Appendix I, *The Role of Secondary Education in a Democratic and Changing Society.*)

Concluding Thoughts

As we approach the 21st century, it is evident that technological progress has far outdistanced progress in human relations. In spite of miracles in technology, science and medicine, when it comes to human relations, it seems at times that we are still living in the dark ages. We find conflict at every level of society—family, neighborhood, city, country, worldwide. It is a luxury we can no longer afford—we never could.

But where do we start? As individuals, we frequently feel overwhelmed in thinking about our nation's or the world's problems. Nevertheless, we can and must contribute by focusing on where we are able to have the most immediate impact—with ourselves, our children, our families, our schools, our neighborhoods and communities.

As we focus on our own children, let us begin by strengthening the bonds between mom and dad—behaving in ways that make each other feel better about ourselves. Simultaneously, we need to extend our love to our children by treating them in the same way. Further, let's involve ourselves in our schools and help to develop in them the same sense of community that we strive for in our families.

Also, we need to extend ourselves outward. We may not have a large extended family, but we can extend our family by loving all children. We need to do this not only because of our humanity, but also because it is in our enlightened self-interest to do so. With millions of children considered at risk in our society, all of us are at risk; as long as this situation continues to exist, no matter how well off we may be, there is no way to protect our children or ourselves from the crime, violence, and chaos that exist in too many of our schools, neighborhoods and cities.

So, yes, we must love not only our own kids but all kids—that includes the kids across the street, on the next block, and on the other side of town. But what does it mean to love all children? Does it have any practical implications? It does not mean that every time we see a kid, we stop him and say, "Hi, I love you." It does mean that we treat all kids in a loving way.

It means that every contact with any child, even a casual contact, is an opportunity to act with courtesy and respect, and not talk down in a patronizing way. It means when you meet a parent and child at a supermarket and greet the parent, you say hello to the child too. When children are in our presence at a dinner or other social gatherings with friends and relatives, we shouldn't ignore them; we should show some interest and include them in some of our conversation without pressuring them to perform in front of others against their will.

At times, we will go further by becoming a mentor, paying for a kid's summer camp trip or deciding to provide ongoing support for a child—perhaps an at-risk child. We might decide to adopt a child or become a foster parent. At another level, we may join efforts to fight hunger, child abuse, drugs, or participate in other children's causes. Once it becomes part of our psyche that we are our brother's keeper—that all children are our children—we will find ways to make more of them a significant part of our thoughts and lives.

Families and schools must join in a partnership to make children our number one priority and, guided by an ethos of love and pragmatism, move vigorously and with determination from talk to action. By creating a positive atmosphere in which people interact with people in ways that make everyone feel respected, important, accepted, included and secure, we can become a powerful force for developing emotionally healthy and high-achieving children, families, and schools— our own and those of others. And, who knows, if enough of us get involved, we might just change the world.

Guide to Parent Resources

(Tools for Life-Long Learning)

f the many excellent publications available on parenting, we have selected a limited number which are particularly useful. They not only represent sound theory but are action-oriented and will facilitate translating theory to action. They include valuable information and a large variety of activities and projects for children to do on their own, with others, or with the entire family. They span all age levels.

For the most part, their selection was made because they support the positive, proactive, preventive approach emphasized in this book rather than a problem, crisis or remedial orientation. However, some will be useful for a specific age group and for dealing with particular problem areas which are beyond the scope of this book. Some are especially inspirational.

Twenty Resources for Learning

(The St. James and Dr. Spock books (#16 and #17) are
hardcover; all others are paperback.)

1. Ames, Louise Bates and Ilg, Frances L. (Series on child
   growth and development with other collaborators: Ha-
   ber, Carol Chase and Baker, Sidney M.)

   Drs. Ames and Ilg are recognized worldwide authorities
   on child behavior and development. Under the auspices
   of the Gesell Institute of Human Behavior, which they
   co-founded in 1950, they have authored an authoritative
   series of 10 volumes on child behavior and development.
   The first 9 books cover ages 1 to 9 (each book 1 year),
   and the tenth deals with ages 10 to 14. These books
   describe the physical, emotional, and psychological development of children in an informative and interesting
   manner, offering much practical and expert advice about
   dealing with child behavior. This series is an outstanding
   resource for helping parents better understand their children at different stages of life.

2. Benson, L., Galbraith, J., Espeland, P. *What Kids Need to
   Succeed.* Minneapolis: Free Spirit Publishing, 1995. (167
   pp., $4.99)

   Based on a nationwide study, this book describes 30
   assets—good things young people need—and over 500
   concrete suggestions to build these assets at home, at
   school, and in the community. These represent a large
   variety of specific activities that can be done alone, with
   family and with others which will contribute to a child's
   sense of accomplishment, self-esteem, and service.

3. Bell, R., and Wildflower, L.Z. *Talking With Your Teenager.* New York: Random House, 1983. (127 pp., $8.95)

The authors emphasize that good communication between parents and teenagers can be facilitated by parents' awareness of what their children are experiencing during adolescence. This book gives detailed information about puberty, emotional health, sexuality, drug/alcohol use and eating disorders, so that parents can discuss these issues with their children knowledgeably and compassionately. They share with readers suggestions from a large number of parents for improving parent-teenager interactions.

4. Boston Women's Health Collective. *Ourselves and Our Children.* New York: Random House, 1978. (288 pp., $9.95)

One of the themes in this book—written collectively by ten women—is that a great gift we can give to our children is a relaxed, happy parent who enjoys life. This book by the Boston Group encourages parents to listen to their own needs, not just as parents but also as people. It explores many important areas such as: How does being a parent relate to the rest of your life—to your own childhood, your work, your relationships, your social and political concerns, your sense of yourself? Where does your support come from? It also contains insights and information gathered from informal interviews with over 200 mothers and fathers.

5. Brazelton, T. Berry. *Touchpoints: Your Child's Emotional and Behavioral Development.* Reading, Mass.: Perseus Books, 1992. (469 pp., $16.00)

Dr. Brazelton is recognized internationally as perhaps the most authoritative expert in the field of child development. His years of experience as a practicing pediatrician, researcher, and teacher uniquely qualifies him to provide parents with an understanding of child development from a physical, cognitive, emotional, and behavioral point of view. *Touchpoints* contains a wealth of information that helps parents deal effectively with childrearing problems, while reducing parents' anxiety and stress and enabling them to prevent future problems.

6. Curran, Dolores. *Traits of a Healthy Family.* New York: Ballantine Books, 1983. (315 pp., $5.99)

The author surveyed 500 professionals—teachers, doctors, pastors, Boy Scout and Girl Scout leaders, social workers and others—to come up with 15 traits most often found in healthy families. Rather than looking at problems, this book focuses on the strength of families. As such, it provides a valuable resource for evaluating the strengths of one's family and is a source of ideas and actions for making it stronger.

7. Davis, L., and Keyser, J. *Becoming the Parent You Want to Be: A Sourcebook of Strategies for the First Five Years.* New York: Broadway Books, 1997. (426 pp., $20)

This is a comprehensive book covering the first five years of childhood. To facilitate the task of lifelong learning, the authors present nine principles to guide the parenting journey. It is a "family friendly" resource which provides much developmental information to help parents understand children's behavior. It offers a wealth of concrete answers to immediate questions related to eating, sleep, discipline, conflict, tantrums, and hundreds of other concerns that arise. It also helps parents define their own goals and use their creativity for problem solving.

8. Gordon, Thomas. *P.E.T. Parent Effectiveness Training: The Tested Way to Raise Responsible Children.* New York: Plume, 1975. (329 pp., $13.95)

This is one of the most widely read and readable books on parent training. First published in 1970, with its clear language and emphasis on specific skills and usable methods, it continues to provide parents practical help in dealing with problems of childrearing and also in preventing them. Parents have learned that they can use the book to develop skills on their own, without necessarily taking P.E.T. classes. Most of the excellent material gives parents additional tools to use in meeting the five critical needs of children.

9. Lazear, J. and Lazear, W. L. *Meditations for Parents Who Do Too Much.* New York: Simon & Schuster, 1993. (365 pp., $9)

This is a small, stimulating book of 365 brief meditations related to the innumerable concerns most parents have or have had at one time or another. It includes much good advice for parents on how to reduce stress on themselves and their children. Although it takes only two or three minutes to read each meditation, you'll find many nuggets of wisdom. It emphasizes slowing down and enjoying parenting more.

10. Lewis, B. A. *The Kid's Guide to Service Projects: Over 500 Service Ideas for Young People Who Want to Make a Difference.* Minneapolis: Free Spirit Publishing, 1995. (175 pp., $10.95)

This is an excellent resource for civic-minded families. Contains over 500 service ideas in areas such as community development, crime fighting, environment, friendship, health, holidays, homelessness, hunger, literacy, people with special needs, politics and government, safety, senior citizens, and transportation. The book also includes a discussion of ten steps for creating successful projects.

11. Lofas, Jeannette, with Sova, Dawn B. *Stepparenting: Everything You Need to Know to Make It Work!* New York: Kensington Books, 1996 (228 pp., $12)

The subtitle tells it all. Anyone who is in a relationship or a marriage which involves children from a previous marriage will find a wealth of information about all aspects of stepparenting. Many issues are discussed which act as barriers to a healthy adult-child relationship, starting with parents' initial dating through establishing a common household and getting married. Many techniques are suggested for solving and preventing problems.

12. Madaras, L. *Talks to Teens About AIDS: An Essential Guide for Parents, Teachers, and Young People.* New York: Newmarket Press, 1988. (106 pp., $5.95)

AIDS is a frightening disease. The thought of it evokes much anxiety and fear among parents and inhibits their ability to discuss it adequately with their children. This book can serve parents, teachers, and teenagers as a tool for understanding and preventing the transmission of this disease. It separates facts from rumors—who gets it, what the symptoms are, how it is and isn't transmitted, and how to prevent it. The book is written in a direct, frank and clear manner and will help parents and teenagers discuss AIDS effectively.

13. Marlor Press. *Kids Vacation Diary*. Saint Paul: Marlor Press, 1995. (95 pp., $6.95)

This is a workbook full of games and activities related to taking a trip, for children from 6-12 years old. These activities take place in three phases: getting ready for the trip, during the trip, memories from the trip. In addition to being fun, the book presents opportunities for improving reading, writing, planning, decision making, and speaking skills. Although written with a vacation trip in mind, the diary can be adapted for home use.

14. Newmark, Gerald. *This School Belongs to You and Me: Every Learner a Teacher, Every Teacher a Learner*. New York: Hart Publishing Company, 1976. (431 pp., $9.95)

This book is a model of innovative education, describing a learning environment from kindergarten through 6th grade where the principal participants—children, parents, teachers and administrators—share responsibility, authority, and accountability in revitalizing the educational process. Four major concepts govern the school; that is, shared learning/teaching (all students become teachers of each other as a central instructional method), shared planning and decision making, shared feedback, and parent/community involvement. (Available through NMI Publishers, Tarzana, CA 91356—800-934-2779.)

15. Peel, Kathy. *The Family Manager's Guide for Working Moms*. New York: Ballantine Books, 1997. (202 pp., $12)

This is an excellent book for parents who want to learn more about organizing their time for maximum efficiency. It shows how to take skills from the business world and transfer them effectively to the home. Lots of ideas, techniques, methods and strategies are presented for working smarter rather than harder. It is not only for working mothers, but also for any busy parent who feels under stress. Adopting even a few of the ideas will yield immediate benefits and lighten the load.

16. St. James, Elaine. *Simplify Your Life With Kids: 100 Ways to Make Life Easier and More Fun.* Kansas City, MO: Andrews McNeel Publishing, 1997. (361 pp., $14.95)

A rich source of ideas for simplifying your life with kids, written in an interesting conversational style. Provides practical, down-to-earth advice on almost every aspect of your life with kids from the time they awaken in the morning until they are fast asleep at night and everything in between. Covers areas such as daily routines, workload, accumulation of "stuff, " telephone management, getting help, family teamwork, simplifying handling of discipline and conflict, simple celebrations, family issues, school and after school, travel, health and much more— all from the point of view of making things easier.

17. Spock, B. M., M.D. *A Better World for Our Children: Rebuilding American Family Values.* Betheseda, MD: National Press Books, 1994. (205 pp., $22.95)

This is a book by the dean of childrearing experts. It empowers parents to influence the future of their children and provides specific activities families can do together to make a difference in their homes and neighborhoods. These activities contribute to family solidarity and to the young person's self-esteem and have many positive by-products.

18. Stock, G. *The Kids Book of Questions.* New York: Workman Publishing, 1988. (207 pp., $4.95)

    Two hundred sixty interesting, thought-provoking questions—includes a few playful ones, too. The questions deal with serious issues and dilemmas that children and adults face throughout life (e.g., dealing with authority, understanding friendship, handling social pressures, overcoming fears, making ethical choices and much more). It can serve as a valuable, weekly or monthly family activity where each member answers a question, followed by discussion.

19. York, P. and York, D. *Tough Love: A Self-Help Manual for Parents Troubled by Teenage Behavior.* Sellersville, PA: Community Service Foundation, 1980.

    This is a manual for parents of teenagers who have serious ongoing problems such as truancy, running away from home, alcohol/drug abuse, trouble with the law. These are the teenagers sometimes considered incorrigible—who have not responded to guidance counselors, caring parents or authority. It is for parents for whom nothing has worked. The manual explains what Toughlove is, who needs it, and spells out a blueprint for putting it into action.

20. Group for Environmental Education, Inc. *Yellow Pages of Learning Resources.* Philadelphia, 1972.

    This is a book concerned with the potential of the city as a place for learning. It calls our urban environments "classrooms without walls" which offer people of all ages endless opportunities. It emphasizes that all the people, places and events of the community at large represent potentially rich resources for learning, which can and should be systematically exploited by our schools. It can also serve as a resource for parents working with their own kids.

REMARKS

The above publications contain a wealth of valuable information about parenting. You will probably want to read a number of the books from cover to cover, skim others, and keep some nearby as references. It would be worthwhile to scan all of them to familiarize yourself with their contents and to identify which ones you might want for a home library. Most can be borrowed from a local library and others can be examined at bookstores.

Family Activities List

Check each item which might be of interest to you. Place a question mark next to any item about which you would like to know more.

Games

___ 20 Questions

___ Board Games (chess, checkers, monopoly, etc.)

___ Cards

___ Charades

___ Crossword Puzzles

___ Darts

___ Dice

___ Horseshoes

___ Jigsaw Puzzles

___ Table Games (pool, billiards)

Sports

___ Archery

___ Badminton

___ Ballooning

___ Baseball

___ Basketball

___ Bicycling

___ Bowling

___ Car Racing/Rallying

___ Croquet

___ Fencing

___ Football

___ Golf

___ Horseback Riding

___ Jogging

___ Judo

___ Kayaking

___ Lawn Bowling

___ Racquet Ball

___ Rowing

___ Sailing

___ Shooting

___ Skating

___ Skateboarding

___ Skiing (Snow, Water)

___ Snorkeling

___ Soccer

___ Sports Viewing

___ Squash

___ Swimming

___ Table Tennis

___ Tennis

___ Volleyball

___ Walking

Nature Activities

___ Animal Care

___ Astronomy

___ Barn Viewing

___ Beachcombing

___ Big Game Hunting

___ Bird Watching

___ Botany

___ Camping

___ Ecology/Conservation

___ Geology

___ Greenhouse Gardening

___ Hiking

___ Indoor Plant Raising

___ Meteorology

___ Mountain Climbing

___ Outdoor Gardening

___ Rock and Fossil Hunting

___ Trapping

___ Tropical Fish Breeding

___ Wild Food Gathering

___ Wildlife Observation

Collecting Activities

___ Antique (Books, Bottles, Dolls, etc.)

___ Buttons

___ Coins

___ Folk Art

___ Fossils

___ Models

___ Photographs (e.g., Airports, City Halls, Amusing Signs)

___ Postcards

___ Posters

___ Recipes

___ Rocks

___ Stamps

Crafts

___ Appliance Repair

___ Automobile Repair

___ Bookbinding

___ Candlemaking

___ Cooking and Baking

___ Decoupage

___ Floral Arranging

___ Furniture

___ Gourmet Cooking

___ House Decorating

___ Kit Assembling

___ Knitting

___ Leather

___ Miniatures

___ Origami

___ Quilting

___ Reupholstery

___ Rugs

___ Sausage Making

___ Scrapbooks

___ Sewing

___ Soldering and Welding

___ Toy Repairing

___ Whittling

___ Wine Making

Art and Music

___ Cartooning

___ Drawing

___ Film Production

___ Group Singing

___ Instrument Playing

___ Joke Telling

___ Lettering

___ Painting

___ Photography

___ Play Acting

___ Play Reading

___ Popular Dancing

___ Puppet Shows

___ Square Dancing

___ Ventriloquism

___ Wood Sculpture

Writing

___ Diary Keeping

___ Fiction Stories

___ Greeting Cards

___ Historical Stories

___ Letter Writing

___ Plays

___ Poetry

___ Short Stories

Social Activities

___ Group Listening

___ Discussion Groups

___ Home Entertaining

___ Visiting Friends

___ Dining Out

___ Picnics

___ Churchgoing

Education, Entertainment, and Cultural Activities

___ Genealogy

___ General Interest College Courses

___ Learning a Foreign Language

___ Reading—General

___ Reading—Special Projects

___ Listening to Classical Music

___ Listening to Popular Music

___ Theater Going

___ Movie Going

___ TV Watching, Analysis, and Evaluation

___ Attending Art Festivals

___ Attending Concerts

___ Visiting Museums

___ Visiting Zoos

___ Special Purpose Field Trips

___ Traveling

___ Going to Auctions

___ Going to Garage Sales and Flea Markets

___ TV Educational Courses

___ Figure and Weight Control

___ Individual Contemplation or Meditation

___ Yoga

___ Exercises

___ Skill Improvement Courses

Volunteer Activities

___ Blind Care

___ Boards of Directors

___ Building Maintenance

___ Children and Youth Group Services

___ Elderly Group Services

___ Foster Home Management

___ Fundraising

___ Library Aides

___ Museum Aides

___ Professional and Managerial Assistance

___ Reading for the Blind

___ Sheltered Workshop Instruction

___ Secretary/Bookkeeping Aides

___ Truck and Car Driving

Organizational Activities

___ Book Clubs

___ Collecting Clubs

___ Communication Clubs

___ Ethnic Organizations

___ Fraternal Organizations

___ Game Clubs

___ Hobby Groups

___ Intercultural Organizations

___ International Aid Groups

___ Nonpartisan Political and Social Action Groups

___ Outdoor Groups

___ Political Groups

___ Religious Groups

___ Service Clubs

___ Sports Clubs

Others

___

___

___

___

___

___

Becoming a Student of My Own Behavior

Keeping A Daily Journal

At the end of the day, *briefly* answer each of the questions below. Create a separate 8 × 11 master sheet of the questions below with enough space for answers and start your own notebook.

1. Which of my actions today were positive in regard to my child's five critical needs? Indicate need and example of action.

2. Which of my actions today were negative in regard to my child's five critical needs? Indicate need and example of action.

3. What did I learn about myself: attitudes, behavior, strengths, weaknesses?

4. If I were doing today over again, what would I do differently?

5. Comments and/or questions about my child's or my attitudes and behavior.

Family Feedback Summary

After the weekly feedback session, *briefly* answer the following questions. Create a separate 8 × 11 master sheet with space for answers and start your own notebook.

1. Was there anything you especially liked about the meeting?

2. Anything you especially disliked about the meeting?

3. Was anything mentioned that detracts from or contributes to family life?

4. Does anything mentioned in #3 above merit further attention?

5. Would you like to do anything differently at the next session?

6. Do any theme(s) persist from week to week that require special attention? (Complete at the end of the fourth session of the month.)

Parent Self-Care Survey

Complete this survey as basis for preparing a personal self-care plan. Create a separate 8 × 11 master sheet of the form below with enough space for answers and start your own notebook.

1. List below the activities you participate in for **personal** pleasure, health, learning. For each activity, indicate frequency and time; desire to do the same, less or more; whether by self, with spouse or others.

ACTIVITY   TIME/FREQUENCY   Same/Less/More   Self/Spouse/Others

2. List any new activities you desire to add (or to replace any of above).

ACTIVITY   TIME/FREQUENCY   Self/Spouse/Others

3. Indicate below persons with whom you socialize (other than spouse) and your desire for the same, less or more time. List any new persons you wish to add (or to replace any of above).

PERSON(S)   TIME/FREQUENCY   Same/Less/More

4. Use the above information to prepare an initial plan. Make a preliminary schedule for 3, 6, or 12 months, subject to change along the way. At the end of the period, update plan and recommit.

Parent Self-Care Evaluation

At the end of each month, *briefly* answer the following questions to assess (1) progress in establishing a balanced lifestyle, and (2) the need to make changes in the plan. Create a separate 8 × 11 master sheet of the questions below with enough space for answers and start your own notebook.

1. To what extent was the plan implemented?

2. What helped or hindered successful implementation of the plan?

3. What did you learn about yourself in regard to self-care: attitudes, behavior, strengths, weaknesses?

4. What changes are needed for the following month, either in the plan or in your behavior?

5. Comments and/or questions.

Family Activities Survey

Complete this survey as basis for preparing a familiy activities plan. Create a separate 8 × 11 master sheet of the form below with enough space for answers and start your own notebook.

1. List below the activities you participate in as a family. For each activity, indicate frequency and time; desire to do the same, less or more; which family members.

ACTIVITY   TIME/FREQUENCY   Same/Less/More   Family Members

2. List any new activities you desire to add (or to replace any of above).

ACTIVITY   TIME/FREQUENCY   Family Members

3. Use the above information to prepare an initial plan. Make a preliminary schedule for 3, 6, or 12 months, subject to change along the way. At the end of the period, update plan and recommit.

Family Activities Evaluation

At the end of each month, *briefly* answer the following questions to assess (1) progress in implementing plan, and (2) the need to make changes in plan or self. Create a separate 8 × 11 master sheet and start your own notebook.

1. To what extent was the plan implemented?

2. What helped or hindered successful implementation of the plan?

3. What did you learn about yourself in regard to family activities: attitudes, behavior, strengths, weaknesses?

4. What changes are needed for the following month, either in the plan or in your behavior?

5. Comments and/or questions.

Children's Well-Being Survey

Complete weekly or monthly for each child. For each item, circle number (or X) as estimate of how well child is doing. Duplicate form and start your own notebook.

Child_____   Date_____

	Not Well (Negative)			Well (Positive)			Not Sure
1. Health	1	2	3	4	5	6	X
a. Sleeping	1	2	3	4	5	6	X
b. Eating	1	2	3	4	5	6	X
c. Exercise	1	2	3	4	5	6	X
d. Energy	1	2	3	4	5	6	X
e. Illness	1	2	3	4	5	6	X
2. Attitudes/Behavior	1	2	3	4	5	6	X
a. Attitude towards life	1	2	3	4	5	6	X
b. Attitude towards people	1	2	3	4	5	6	X
c. Attitude towards family life	1	2	3	4	5	6	X
d. Self-respect	1	2	3	4	5	6	X
e. Respect for others	1	2	3	4	5	6	X
f. Self-confidence	1	2	3	4	5	6	X
g. Trust in others	1	2	3	4	5	6	X
h. Feels valued	1	2	3	4	5	6	X
i. Shows gratitude	1	2	3	4	5	6	X
j. Feels included	1	2	3	4	5	6	X
k. Includes others	1	2	3	4	5	6	X
l. Helpfulness	1	2	3	4	5	6	X
3. Leisure/Recreation Activities	1	2	3	4	5	6	X
4. Relationships	1	2	3	4	5	6	X
a. Parents	1	2	3	4	5	6	X
b. Brothers/Sisters	1	2	3	4	5	6	X
c. Other family members	1	2	3	4	5	6	X
d. Friends	1	2	3	4	5	6	X
e. Boy/Girl	1	2	3	4	5	6	X
5. Learning/School	1	2	3	4	5	6	X
6. Use of Time	1	2	3	4	5	6	X

Role of Secondary Education in a Democratic and Changing Society

Secondary education occupies that portion of a person's life which may be characterized as the period of transition from adolescence to adulthood. Becoming an adult signifies taking more responsibility for one's own life, making more decisions on one's own (especially significant personal decisions concerning work, recreation, education, relations with the opposite sex), becoming self-supporting financially, and generally moving from dependency to independence. It also should mean assuming more responsibility for improving the quality of life in the community and becoming a more active participant in the democratic processes of society.

Secondary education, therefore, is in the business of "growing adults." In doing so, it must consider the needs of the individual and of the community. Adolescent needs to explore, have choices, develop interests, and achieve confidence, competence and a sense of self-worth. The community needs individuals of integrity who are cooperative, caring and civic-minded.

One of the problems in achieving an effective transition from adolescence to adulthood has been the relative isolation and segregation of the young from adult activities. Another has been the constraints inherent in confining education to the schoolhouse and in the traditional structure of large group, lock-step instruction with the teacher as the sole disseminator of information and the student as the passive recipient. Further, the hierarchical, autocratic nature of most schools has created adversarial rather than cooperative relations among school participants. Instead of the school being the most interesting and exciting environment in every community, too often students, teachers, and administrators are bored, frustrated, unhappy and angry.

To "grow adults" the school itself must grow up. The secondary school must become a learning community with its various members joined in a common effort to improve the learning of all. Graduates of this type of community should be recognized by their capability for self-directed study; ability to work cooperatively and effectively with peers; positive attitudes towards learning; high levels of competence in selected areas of the curriculum; confidence in their ability to learn new things; concern for the growth, development and well-being of others, and readiness to succeed in higher education or in the work force.

Major Goal Areas

ACQUISITION OF KNOWLEDGE AND SKILLS

Secondary education should assist students in acquiring the knowledge and skills necessary to function effectively in society and to understand and enjoy the world about them. (The knowledge and skills described below are not all-inclusive but give a sense of emphasis.)

By age eighteen every student should have developed competence in the basic communication skills of listening, speaking, reading and writing. Opportunities should be provided both to make up for past deficiencies and to progress to more advanced levels of communication skills, technical and creative writing. Since these basic skills are essential to continuing one's education, to entering the work world, and to effective citizenship, they should be emphasized in all areas of the curriculum.

In addition to the basic skills and the minimal information that every student would acquire in the arts and sciences and humanities as preparation for college or as part of his general knowledge, secondary education should enable every student to achieve competence or mastery in several areas, whether or not he continues with his formal education. Every student should develop proficiency in an occupation that may be filled by a high school graduate. He should be equipped to begin earning a living on a part-time or full-time basis. Every student should choose one academic subject in which he would concentrate efforts. Every student should engage in some *individual* sport which could provide lifelong exercise and enjoyment. Every student should be encouraged to develop appreciation for art or music and provided with an opportunity to become proficient in some aspect of either.

In addition to developing an appreciation for good health, each student should plan and participate in an individual exercise program, earning a minimum of thirty aerobics points per week. One of the most important, rewarding and perhaps most difficult areas of life is that of relationships with the opposite sex. Yet, students have little preparation for courtship, sexual relations, marriage, parenthood. Opportunities to question, study, learn and discuss should be provided throughout secondary education.

CAPABILITY FOR SELF-DIRECTED LEARNING

In the age of "future shock" everything changes constantly and the only constant is change itself. New information becomes dated or obsolete almost as fast as it is discovered. Technological advances often carry with them the seed of future problems. Effective functioning requires the ability to learn continually throughout one's life. Under these conditions, self-directed learning is an important educational objective. The self-directed learner is able to formulate his own goals, consider alternatives, prepare a plan, choose and utilize material and human resources effectively, evaluate his own progress, revise plans, work at a task independently, and persist long enough to bring them to fruition.

INTERPERSONAL RELATIONS
AND A SENSE OF COMMUNITY

Our society has tremendous problems as witnessed by ever-increasing school dropouts, vandalism, divorce rate, drug abuse, crime and violence in the streets, dishonesty in government, and race relations.

Most of our problems are not technical problems but are people problems. We do not seem to be able to get along with each other, to trust, to communicate, to care, to work together. People helping people is no longer a luxury but a matter of survival.

Secondary education should develop skills in working cooperatively with others, and in developing a sense of ownership in our institutions. Schools should foster cooperation over competition, teamwork over adversarial relations. The school should become a learning community with each classroom a micro-community.

Methodology

INDIVIDUALIZED INSTRUCTION

The ratio of one teacher to thirty or more students makes it almost impossible to attend to the wide range of individual differences in aptitude, abilities, motivation, learning styles and achievement levels. Material and methods should allow each student to progress at his own pace, receive individual help when, where, and how he needs it. These have been available for some time in the form of cross-age student tutoring, programmed instruction, computer-assisted learning and other self-teaching material; smaller class size; volunteers in the classroom, and big brother and mentor programs. Nevertheless, their implementation in schools across the nation has not been widespread or consistent.

STUDENT TUTORING

Learning by teaching, or peer and cross-age student tutoring, is an important method of individualizing instruction and is also highly motivating. As a recipient, the student receives individual help; as a tutor, the student sharpens his own learning skills.

Secondary education should promote the broad notion of the helping relationship within every classroom and across grade levels. This is not a remedial approach, but rather one in which all students become resources for one another by working in teams. Everyone learns to teach and teaches to learn.

Student tutoring helps develop a sense of community, caring and responsibility. Being placed in a position of responsibility motivates the tutor and makes him feel important. Assisting other children to learn helps him test, develop, and internalize his own knowledge. It gives the tutor insights into the learning process. Competition is replaced by cooperation.

SHARED PLANNING AND DECISION MAKING

Our nation prides itself in its democratic institutions, yet we attempt to prepare young people for active participation as citizens without offering them adequate opportunity to learn and practice the necessary skills.

The secondary school should be a vibrant, living-learning community, where students develop a sense of ownership by participating in governing and running the school. Students, parents, and staff should jointly establish goals and plan and carry them out. As students develop a sense of proprietorship, vandalism, absenteeism, dropouts, underachieving and apathy will decrease, and be replaced by interest, excitement, participation, caring, and concern. Students become turned on to school and to one another.

TASK-ORIENTED FEEDBACK

No matter how much cohesiveness exists at the outset among professional practitioners (teachers and administrators) and the clients (children and parents) conflicts will appear, especially as circumstances change. The test of character of any organization or community is not the absence of differences but rather how these are handled. Mishandled, they become destructive to the educational process. Handled well, they become a positive force for effective change. Thus, the school must have built-in provisions for self-criticism and self-correction. The task-oriented feedback session is such a mechanism.

Task-oriented group feedback is an opportunity through regular, open, discussion to understand the effects one's actions have on others and vice versa. It is a time when people can share problems and ask for and offer help. It is an exercise in self-government where all decisions and actions can be questioned, including those of persons in authority. It is an occasion to share views honestly, in a non-threatening atmosphere, a place where people do not respond defensively to criticism but welcome it as a means of learning and clearing the air.

Feedback sessions are generally unstructured and without any agenda. The basic question addressed is: "What do we see each other doing that is either hindering or helping us achieve the school's objectives and maintain a high morale?"

COMMUNITY AS A CLASSROOM

A major problem mentioned in achieving an effective transition from adolescence to adulthood is the relative isolation of the young from important adult activities. One of the ways of changing this is through the concept of the "community as a classroom."

This concept emphasizes that all the people, places, and events of the community at large represent potentially rich and important resources for learning which can and should be systematically exploited. The "Yellow Pages of Learning Resources," a manual concerned with the potential of the city as a place for learning, states: "Education has been thought of as taking place mainly within the confines of the classroom, and school buildings have been regarded as the citadels of knowledge. However, the most extensive facility imaginable for learning is our urban environment. It is a classroom without walls, an open university for people of all ages offering a boundless curriculum with unlimited expertise. If we can make our urban environment comprehensible and observable, we will have created classrooms with endless windows on the world."

As the city becomes a classroom and the skills of parents and community people become available to the school, the isolation of youth will be broken down.

Summing Up

An important reason that schools are failing—and even the most successful are underachieving—is the lack of a sense of community and a feeling of powerlessness. Money, materials, equipment, and new buildings, while important and necessary, will have limited impact on results as long as children, parents, teachers, and administrators feel powerless and experience themselves as victims or adversaries. The school must have a cohesive philosophy and program around which enthusiasm, energy and support can be mobilized.

The secondary school should attempt to become a "learning community," characterized by the feeling that problems are "our problems," failures are "our failures," and successes "our successes." This is based on the idea that people learn, grow, participate, and contribute best in a situation where they feel they have some control over their own destinies.

Students should acquire intellectual and vocational competence, a sense of self-worth, the ability to learn on their own, concern for the well-being of others, and skill in working cooperatively. This should enable students to face the future with confidence and excitement, whether they continue their formal education or enter the world of work.

Index of
Chapter Contents

INTRODUCTION
(Challenges of Parenting: Pleasures, Paradoxes, Pitfalls)   1

1. THE FIVE CRITICAL NEEDS OF CHILDREN   9
    (Parenting as Though Children Really Matter)

Need to Feel Respected   10
    Rudeness, Discourtesy   11
    Lying   12
    Demeaning Behavior   13
    Interrupting/Ignoring/Half-Listening   14
    Summing Up   14

Need to Feel Important   15
    Overprotectiveness   16
    Excessive Permissiveness   16
    Talking Too Much/Not Listening   17
    Decision Making/Problem Solving   18
    Responsibility/Authority   19
    Summing Up   19

Need to Feel Accepted   20
   Overreacting/Emotionality   21
   Suppressing Feelings   22
   Being Overly Critical   23
   Positive Reinforcement   24
   Summing Up   24
Need to Feel Included   25
   Activities   26
   Worklife Activity   26
   Decisions   26
   Discussions   27
   Family Feedback Meetings   27
   Summing Up   29
Need to Feel Secure   29
   Relationship of Parents With Each Other   30
   A Caring, Affectionate Environment   30
   Tradition and Rituals   31
   Discipline   31
      Responsibility for Actions   31
      Excessive Limits   32
      Excessive/Inappropriate Punishment   32
      Inconsistent Punishment   33
      Physical Punishment   33
      Self-Discipline   34
   Summing Up   34
What About Love?   35
Concluding Thoughts   36

2. FAMILY SITUATIONS 39
(A Closer Look at Behavior That Helps
and Behavior That Hurts)

Family Situations 39

SITUATION 1: Respect, Acceptance 40
(To Buy or Not to Buy?—
A Shakespearean Dilemma)

SITUATION 2: Acceptance, Respect 41
(Music Lover's Taste)

SITUATION 3: Inclusion, Respect, Security 43
(Parental Secrecy)

SITUATION 4: Respect, Importance 44
(My Room, My Castle)

SITUATION 5: Respect, Security 46
(Grandma and Grandpa Know Best—
or Do They?)

SITUATION 6: Security, Inclusion, Acceptance 48
(Parents' Divorce)

SITUATION 7: Acceptance, Inclusion,
Importance 49
(Changing Baby's Diaper)

SITUATION 8: Acceptance, Security 51
(To Let The Bird Fly Or Not)

SITUATION 9: Acceptance, Respect, Security 53
(Forced Piano Playing)

SITUATION 10: Security, Inclusion,
Importance 54
(Siblings Fighting/Parents' Despair)

SITUATION 11: Acceptance, Security 56
(Sex and the Pre-Teenager)

SITUATION 12: Inclusion   58
(A Failure To Communicate!)

SITUATION 13: Acceptance, Security   59
(Better Late Than Never—or Is It?)

Summing Up   61

3. RECOLLECTIONS FROM CHILDHOOD   63
(Memories Have Impact)

Selected Responses   64

    Respect   64

        Not Feeling Respected   64

        Feeling Respected   65

    Importance   66

        Not Feeling Important   66

        Feeling Important   66

    Acceptance   67

        Not Feeling Accepted   67

        Feeling Accepted   68

    Inclusion   69

        Not Feeling Included   69

        Feeling Included   69

    Security   70

        Not Feeling Secure   70

        Feeling Secure   71

Summing Up   72

4. BECOMING A PROFESSIONAL AT PARENTING   73
(Childrearing Is Too Important to Leave to Chance)

Amateur vs. Professional   74

Elements of Professionalism   74

Making Conscious Decisions 75

Having a Game Plan 75

Becoming a Student of Your Own Behavior 76

Having an Experimental Attitude 77

Applying Elements of Professionalism 78

Making Conscious Decisions 78

Adopting the Five Critical Needs 78

Creating a Balanced Lifestyle 79

Becoming a Professional 79

Having a Game Plan 79

GAME PLAN #1: Ongoing Review
of Basic Concepts 80

GAME PLAN #2: Becoming a Student
of Your Own Behavior 80

GAME PLAN #3: Family Feedback 82

GAME PLAN #4: Emphasizing Positive
Reinforcement 84

GAME PLAN #5: Planning a Family Activity 85

GAME PLAN #6: Establishing Family Rules 86

GAME PLAN #7: Creating Family Traditions 88

GAME PLAN #8: Family Reading/
Storytelling Activity 89

GAME PLAN #9: A Team Approach
to Cooking and Kitchen Work 90

GAME PLAN #10: Family Study
of Meaning and Significance of Respect 92

GAME PLAN #11: Parent Self-Care 92

GAME PLAN #12: Participating in a
Parent Support Group 94

Summing Up 95

5. OVERCOMING OBSTACLES AND
TAKING CONTROL   99
(Maintaining Focus and a Balanced Lifestyle)

Overcoming Obstacles   99

    Feeling Overwhelmed   99

    Neglect of Planning   100

    Resistance to Planning   100

        Cultural Conditioning   101

        Myth of Spontaneity   101

        Advantages of Being Overwhelmed   102

    Over-Seriousness   102

    Unrealistic Expectations   103

Taking Control of Your Life   104

    Prepare Preliminary To-Do List   104

    Prioritize and Schedule   105

    Creating Additional Time   105

    Ongoing Planning and Revision   108

Summing Up   108

6. IMPLICATIONS FOR FAMILIES AND SCHOOLS   111
(Creating and Extending a Sense of Community)

Families   111

    A Sense of Community   111

        Core Values   112

        Self-Sacrifice/Self-Care   113

        Making It Happen   114

    First Five Years of Life   114

    Teenagers   115

    Significant Others   117

Single-Parent Families 117
Parents in Second Marriages 117
Summing Up 118
Schools 120
Schools and the Five Critical Needs 120
Concluding Thoughts 121

7. GUIDE TO PARENT RESOURCES 125
(Tools for Life-Long Learning)
Twenty Resources for Learning 126
Remarks 134

About the Author

GERALD NEWMARK, Ph.D., president of the Newmark Management Institute, is a parent, educator, behavioral scientist, and management consultant. Throughout his career, Dr. Newmark has employed a combination of common sense and the scientific method to help organizations and individuals become more effective.

For 15 years, he was a Human Factors Scientist with System Development Corporation where his work focused on the design, development, and evaluation of innovative training and instructional systems for public schools and military programs.

Under a seven-year Ford Foundation grant, Dr. Newmark worked with children, parents, and teachers in Los Angeles city schools as co-director of a project to develop a model school. The results of this effort are described in his book, *This School Belongs to You and Me: Every Learner a Teacher, Every Teacher a Learner.* For this work, Dr. Newmark received a presidential citation.

An important aspect of Dr. Newmark's adult life has been participation in civic and youth affairs. He was involved for six years with the Synanon Foundation in its pioneering work in the treatment of drug addiction, and with Operation Bootstrap in Central Los Angeles in projects to improve inter-racial relations. He has been a consultant to the California Special Olympics and the California State Department of Education. Dr. Newmark has served on the advisory boards of the National Commission on Resources for Youth, and two drug abuse programs—Amity, Inc. in Arizona, and Tuum Est in Los Angeles.

Dr. Newmark is a member of the American Association of Humanistic Psychology, the Charles F. Menninger Society, and the National Association for the Mentally Ill. He presently serves on the Board of Directors of two non-profit organizations: The Catticus Corporation and The Center for Reuniting Families.

The Children's Project

The Children's Project is a grass-roots, non-commercial effort initiated by Dr. Gerald Newmark and Deborah Newmark to help parents, families, teachers and all childcare providers create the emotional foundation necessary for children to be successful at school and in life. The principal resource used in this effort is Dr. Newmark's book "How To Raise Emotionally Healthy Children: Meeting the Five Critical Needs of Children...And Parents Too!" It is available in both English and Spanish. The Newmark Management Institute makes books available to groups and organizations at the low case price of $2.10 per book, tax and delivery included (case price $159.60 for 76 books).

Dr. Newmark advises schools, health organizations, corporations, and other groups on establishing effective parent support groups. He also conducts training workshops for individuals who lead such groups or are teachers in parent education programs. In addition, Dr. Newmark makes frequent presentations and keynote addresses at school, childcare provider, child advocate, parent education and corporate events. There are no fees for speaking engagements, training workshops, consulting services, or teaching guides available for use with the book.

For information contact Deborah Newmark, Director
818/708-1244   nmipub@earthlink.net

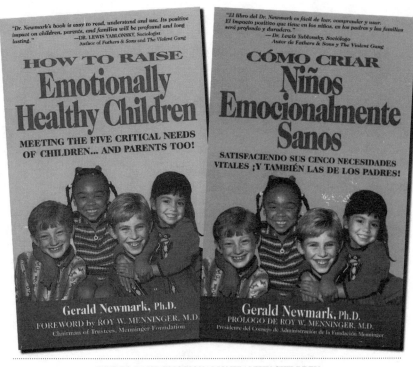

HOW TO RAISE EMOTIONALLY HEALTHY CHILDREN
by Gerald Newmark, Ph.D.
ORDER FORM

Contact Person

Company/Organization

Address

City   State   Zip

Telephone   Fax

E-mail address

Publisher: NMI Publishers, 18653 Ventura Blvd., #547, Tarzana, CA 91356
Tel. 818/708-1244, Fax: 818/345-3249, E-mail: nmipub@earthlink.net

Retail Price $11.95
SPECIAL CASE PRICING:

$2.10 PER BOOK (price includes tax & delivery)
(English Edition 76 books per case)
(Spanish Edition 76 books per case)

[Lower prices are available for large quantities.]

# of Cases (English edition) _____
   Price (@$159.60 per case) $_____

# of Cases (Spanish edition) _____
   Price (@$159.60 per case) $_____

Total $_____

Mail check or money order to: NMI Publishers
18653 Ventura Blvd., #547, Tarzana, CA 91356

Individual copies can be purchased from Amazon.com or through your local bookstore (Retail Price: $11.95)
English version ISBN#0-932767-07-9, Spanish version ISBN#0-932767-08-07